Stumbling through
Space and Time

of related interest

Caged in Chaos
A Dyspraxic Guide to Breaking Free
Victoria Biggs
Illustrated by Sharon Tsang
Foreword by Jo Todd
ISBN 978 1 84905 474 4
eISBN 978 0 85700 873 2

All About Dyspraxia
Understanding Developmental Coordination Disorder
Kathy Hoopmann
ISBN 978 1 78775 835 3
eISBN 978 1 78775 836 0

The Dyslexia, ADHD, and DCD-Friendly Study Skills Guide
Tips and Strategies for Exam Success
Ann-Marie McNicholas
ISBN 978 1 78775 177 4
eISBN 978 1 78775 178 1

The Spectrum Girl's Survival Guide
How to Grow Up Awesome and Autistic
Siena Castellon
Foreword by Temple Grandin
ISBN 978 1 78775 183 5
eISBN 978 1 78775 184 2

STUMBLING THROUGH SPACE and TIME

Living Life with Dyspraxia

Rosemary Richings

Jessica Kingsley Publishers
London and Philadelphia

First published in Great Britain in 2023 by Jessica Kingsley Publishers
An imprint of Hodder & Stoughton Ltd
An Hachette Company

1

The fonts, layout and overall design of this book have been prepared
according to dyslexia friendly principles. At JKP we aim to make our
books' content accessible to as many readers as possible.

The information contained in this book is not intended to replace the services
of trained medical professionals or to be a substitute for medical advice. You
are advised to consult a doctor on any matters relating to your health, and in
particular on any matters that may require diagnosis or medical attention.

A CIP catalogue record for this title is available from the
British Library and the Library of Congress

ISBN 978 1 83997 269 0
eISBN 978 1 83997 270 6

Printed and bound in the United States by Integrated Books International

Jessica Kingsley Publishers' policy is to use papers that are natural, renewable
and recyclable products and made from wood grown in sustainable
forests. The logging and manufacturing processes are expected to
conform to the environmental regulations of the country of origin.

Jessica Kingsley Publishers
Carmelite House
50 Victoria Embankment
London EC4Y 0DZ

www.jkp.com

To Erin Gilmer and every disabled advocate just like
her. Erin was a courageous fighter for the justice
of disabled people. Her story must live on.

*"For disabled people to thrive, we need webs of help, support,
understanding, and care. But in an able-bodied literary
world, we are all expected to succeed on our own, never to
need assistance. Until we change that paradigm, it will be
incredibly hard for most disabled people to finish and send
out their work into the world."* —A.H. Reaume (2019)

Erin never got to finish the work she started,
but I will, and I will never take for granted any
opportunity that I get to share my work.

Contents

Introduction

In the many years that have passed since my dyspraxia diagnosis, it's been rare for me to talk to anyone who reacts to my disability with anything besides confusion. So, let's start with a quick definition. Dyspraxia is a disability that gives me an underdeveloped sense of space, time, and coordination. On an average day, I react to verbal instructions and the limitations of my environment at a slower rate than my peers. As a result, I can't process verbal instructions and conversations in environments that are too noisy, busy, or filled with too many sensory distractions. Another key attribute of my disability is my lack of fine and gross motor skills. Activities like team sports, arts and crafts, and learning a new dance routine are a challenge (CanChild, 2020).

No matter how many times people try to explain it to me, I constantly mix up the difference between up and down, left and right. I also misjudge how much time is needed to travel to specific locations and get lost easily. To compensate for my lack of navigation skills, I have a photographic memory of minor details of streets, landmarks, and buildings. Many of my peers might see the color of an awning or graffiti on a statue once and forget about it. I, however, remember exactly what a street or statue I only saw once looks like decades later.

Because globally there is a lack of awareness of dyspraxia, you might think that dyspraxia is a rare neurodevelopmental disorder, but it's more common than you might think. In fact, GMB Union called dyspraxia a "workplace issue" that affects (an estimated) 5 percent of the population (Turner & Andrew, 2020).[1]

When did I get diagnosed, and what was my life like back then?

In 1994, I was diagnosed with dyspraxia, and I was unable to do all the things that children are expected to do by the time they're in school. For me, this included everything from riding a bike and catching a ball, to reading, writing, and basic math. According to a family legend, I couldn't even understand why an orange (as in the fruit) was orange.

I asked my father why I had medical tests pre-diagnosis, and he recalled an incident when I lost control of my balance and fell down the stairs, although it likely had something to do with everyone's concerns about how slowly I was learning how to get dressed, walk, and tie my shoelaces without help (Harris, Mickelson, & Zwicker, 2015). Then, once I finally learned how to write, additional challenges emerged. Holding a pen or pencil in my hands was extremely painful and no one could read my handwriting. Gripping my pen and squeezing it tightly in between my middle and index fingers was the only way I could write. Otherwise, my pen would fall out of my hand mid-sentence. So, my parents did what most logical parents would do and took me to the doctor.

I got sent to several specialists at a major Canadian children's hospital;[2] I had blood tests, MRIs, appointments with physiotherapists and occupational therapists, speech pathology testing, and psychological assessments (Biotteau et al., 2019). I hated every minute of it. Being outside in the sunshine

---

1   Since dyspraxia is heavily underdiagnosed, the exact number of people is not known—no one knows for sure how many undiagnosed or misdiagnosed children, youth, and adults are "out there."

2   The Hospital for Sick Children in Toronto.

seemed a lot more appealing than sitting in a sterile hospital waiting room. Several appointments later, my parents received a phone call from the family doctor announcing my diagnosis: dyspraxia.

I don't remember how I found out about it, but it was probably handled a bit like how my father tells me about a death in the family. He waits until I'm comfortably seated, as his Oxfordshire accent suddenly includes an aura of soft gentleness. Then, he explains what this means for me and everyone else we care about.

In the Canadian big city region of Toronto that I grew up in, 1994 was also the year of budget cuts to healthcare and education. The medical team responsible for my diagnosis had to test and diagnose me with limited resources. It was a slow process, and all my parents got was an outdated pamphlet on clumsy child syndrome.[3]

When I was diagnosed, my mother was reading a book about a man who has prosopagnosia, a medical condition where you cannot recognize faces. Learning more about someone who has a neurological condition that makes him see the world differently helped her understand what having a daughter who also sees the world differently for similar reasons could be like. More recently, my dad recommended a movie called The Last Detail, where Randy Quaid's character is neurodiverse. He told me it influenced him a great deal when he was a young man, and it was his first introduction to neurodiversity.

On a global level, there are so many dyspraxics with stories that deserve to be told, but I think that you'll be interested in my story for one very important reason: I have known that I have dyspraxia, otherwise known as developmental coordination

---

3   Clumsy child syndrome is a synonym for dyspraxia that isn't used anymore. When you use this term, you're assuming that the symptoms are something that children will outgrow. This couldn't be more inaccurate: dyspraxia is a permanent condition.

disorder (DCD),[4] for as long as I can remember. I never had to figure out how dyspraxia affected who I am as a person, because it has always been a background presence in my life. My peers bullied and teased me when I was in school, and it made me wish that I had never received a diagnosis. Once I struggled with other health issues, I no longer felt that way. If you haven't developed good coping mechanisms, your chances of thriving are lower.

Good coping mechanisms take practice, and don't happen immediately. Dyspraxics are born with their disability, but dyspraxia is the underrepresented sibling of neurodevelopmental conditions such as autism and attention deficit hyperactivity disorder (ADHD). Autism and ADHD have been a lot more heavily studied, written about, and recognized in the medical community. Far too many dyspraxics and their families must figure out how to live with dyspraxia on their own, and growing up with dyspraxia is complicated. Everything from first dates to first jobs is awkward and acceptance is never a guarantee.

This isn't an "inspiration" story, a trope in storytelling that I openly mock. Inspiration stories treat people with disabilities like a one-dimensional representation of their disability. I'm proud to say that I am so much more than a person with dyspraxia.

I'm a self-employed university graduate, wife, and proud contributor to the lives and wellbeing of my family. I've developed websites and blog posts for numerous businesses, have my own blog, and have been a trusted social media marketing resource for so many different people. In the early days of my diagnosis, I had a lot less to feel proud of, and I felt like my family's biggest burden.

---

4   Developmental coordination disorder is the clinical diagnostic term, but people with lived experience often prefer *dyspraxia*, although I have often used DCD in medical settings to help practitioners understand why I am reacting to my environment in a specific way. The terms DCD and dyspraxia are used interchangeably in this book.

My approach to writing this book

This book attempts the difficult task of looking back on years of lived experience. However, memory is never a perfect source of information. To solve this problem, the information disclosed in this book has been verified through conversations with people who were there, several hours of research, copies of my medical records, and personal diary entries. To prevent this book from only focusing on my own experiences, I have also spoken to disabled people of diverse backgrounds, ages, and life experiences.

As an avid traveler and person who grew up in a multicultural city, I have listened to the stories of disabled people who grew up in North America, the U.K., and a wide variety of European countries, along with the Middle East and India. Many of the topics explored in this book are a direct response to the conversations I have had with the people I have met so far.

> Please note some names have been changed throughout to protect anonymity.

PART I

GROWING UP WITH DYSPRAXIA

"For years I was harshly judged and misunderstood. Because I wasn't learning complex movements and sports activities at the same pace as everyone else."

—from my Medium Digest article about the challenges of staying fit as a neurodiverse person (Richings, 2020a)

Chapter 1

What Happens After You're Diagnosed?

In my first few years of knowing that I had dyspraxia, my most important role model was my elder brother. When he was still living at home, we spent a lot of time together. My brother and I were so close that medical professionals, eager to help me through my diagnosis process, included my brother in every step of the therapy process.

My brother's earliest memory of my dyspraxia was his extensive participation in the Wilbarger Protocol. According to National Autism Resources (2021):

> The Wilbarger Protocol (also referred to as brushing therapy) is often a part of a sensory therapy program. It involves brushing the body with a small surgical brush throughout the day. People who exhibit symptoms of tactile defensiveness are extremely sensitive to touch.

The Wilbarger Protocol was pitched to my parents as a solution to my issues with sensory processing (sensory processing disorder). Lisa Jo Rudy (2020), a VeryWell Health website contributor, says: "Many practitioners regard it as a singular condition and there are even clinics that specifically treat it. At the same time, however, sensory processing disorder is not in the Diagnostic and Statistical Manual of Mental Disorders (DSM-5)."

Occupational therapists (and some pediatricians) recognize and treat sensory processing disorder, but a lot of psychiatrists still don't consider it to be a diagnosable condition. However, sensory processing issues are still important to talk about because they are something that a lot of dyspraxics experience. In 2017, the *British Journal of Occupational Therapy* published a study of 93 children with DCD. When the study was complete, researchers learned that most of the children who participated in the study had difficulties with sensory processing and integration that affected their everyday life (Allen & Casey, 2017).

How do sensory processing issues affect me?

Certain sounds, lights, and textures cause my energy to drain very quickly. When that happens, my dyspraxia symptoms will be a lot more severe than usual (Engel-Yeger & Segal, 2018). Then anxiety will impair my judgment and I'll get intense headaches. When my sensory processing issues happen, functions like sleep, focus, and ability to react to the limitations of my environment are disrupted or non-existent. Retreating to a quiet environment for a while, dimming the lights, and resting make a huge difference. This was an aspect of my disability I noticed before my parents, but I didn't tell them about it because I had no idea how to explain it to them.

I remember a Halloween trick-or-treating experience where I processed more sensory input than I could handle. There were flashing lights, battery-powered plastic ghosts lunging in the direction of passersby, a person dressed up as a werewolf scaring kids, a lot of different noises at the same time, and big crowds of children. Before I could get close enough to get any candy, I hyperventilated, and tears ran down my face as I ran toward my mom.

Wilbarger Protocol (brushing therapy): What I thought of it

This brushing therapy was sold to my family as some sort of cure or magic pill solution. To maximize the effects of the brushing therapy, an occupational therapist taught my brother and the rest of my family the steps required to conduct the therapy without the assistance of a practitioner. It was unpleasant at first, but the only reason I cooperated was because my brother was an extremely persuasive participant in the brushing therapy process. There was no one I trusted more than my brother at the time. So even though I hated the process, I committed to it until the very end.

Every two hours, eight times a day, and for several weeks, my brother would use a plastic brush to brush me from head to toe. This process would typically happen in a circular scrubbing motion and build up sensory defensiveness. The brush that was used closely resembled the brushes I've seen at dog groomers and stables. The bristles are soft and coated in soft silicone. Since some of this process happened during the school day, my brother had an automatic hall pass to leave class every two hours to "brush" his sister.

Rather than any kind of cure or solution, I would describe the Wilbarger Protocol more as something that made sensory overload go from unmanageable to something I could at least psychologically talk myself through if I had no other choice but to face it. It does not replace the very real need for resting and doing whatever it takes to rejuvenate your energy when exceeding the limits of what you can realistically handle. To this day, I have moments where I tire myself from processing more sensory input than I can handle, and that's when it's something that I cannot ignore for a moment longer.

What you need to know about stimming

Due to my sensory processing issues, I share one thing in common with autistic people, a tendency to stim. Stimming is the body language of people with sensory disabilities. Hand flapping, rocking back and forth, spinning objects, visual stimming, auditory stims, verbal stims, and pressure stims are some of the ways it happens.

For me, stimming happens through chronic arm, hand, and leg twitching and flapping. I also grab both hands, squeeze them tightly, and spin my hands in circles a lot. When I'm stressed, excited, or anxious, I do everything I just mentioned without being consciously aware of it. Although sometimes it happens when I'm hyper-focused on something.

Eventually, I got my first stim toys, gentle, brightly colored children's toys made from soft elastic. My stim toys made it possible for me to train my brain to grab the objects instead of risking hurting myself by accident. Sometimes, I squeeze my hand too tightly without realizing. When this happens, my grip is so strong that I risk hurting my wrist if I'm unable to access my stim toys.

If you are a stimmer, you may be wondering which stim toy is best for you. A lot just depends on what type of stimmer you are, and what sensory input you are the most sensitive to. For me, circular stim toys are great because I can easily shake, twirl, and throw them in between my hands. I also often hide a small keyring with a few plastic beads on it in my pocket for occasions when I want to stim by pushing the beads in various directions without anyone knowing that's what I'm doing. At neurodivergent community social events I have attended, I have come across stimmers who put objects in their mouth and suck on them, and those who use stim toys that make a noise in reaction to not enough stimuli. Some more subtle stim behavior I have seen is rocking back and forth, which rarely involves a stim toy of any kind.

I recommend looking for objects made of strong, difficult-to-break materials like silicone, elastic, and metal. That way, you will have a low risk of breaking or swallowing your stim toy when you're stressed out, tired, and experiencing sensory overload.

How I learned to catch and throw a ball

Without instruction or supervision, my brother developed his own approach to teaching me the motor skills that you need to thrive in the average playground. In a way, it was all about priorities. He wanted to be able to throw a ball back and forth with his sister, like most kids really. I couldn't even hold a pen or pencil or catch a ball, but this didn't stop my brother from having a normal childhood with his sister.

In the earliest photo my parents have of my brother and me, I'm a newborn baby fast asleep in my brother's arms. His eyes are half on me, and half on passersby. This photo perfectly summed up our relationship from day one. He wanted to protect me and expected nothing in return.

The summer after my diagnosis, my family and I went to the beach. My brother wanted to dip his feet in the water, and I followed him. First, he told me to duck, but I didn't know what that meant. Then he crouched down with his head under water. We did this a few more times before he threw a ball in my direction and told me to duck. After several attempts, I ducked just in time. Then he repeated this process when my parents were paying attention, and their immediate reaction was amazement.

My very first occupational therapist

The playground, for me, was a hostile place of danger. The only time I was safe in the playground was when I was reading, walking, and talking with my friends; I was an accident waiting to happen whenever I used the same playground equipment as the other children. When my teachers started to notice that this was an issue, my occupational therapist, Wendy Wallace, started to come to my school and teach me the fine and gross motor skills I was struggling with.

Through getting to know me a little bit better, Wendy Wallace realized that everything else required a process like how my elder brother taught me how to duck and catch a ball. Patient repetition helped me work around my unsteady hand grip of inanimate objects. Once I memorized a cohesive, consistent pattern for tying shoelaces, I could tie them well enough not to trip on my way to school. For pens, pencils, and scissors we took a completely different approach. Writing with pens and pencils hurt my wrist. So, Wendy Wallace made sure I could use foam grips to decrease the pain.

Since this process started in the 1990s, laptops were not yet a "thing." Instead, my parents bought me a vintage typewriter, and I took an instant liking to it. I got very quick, very fast at typing, and memorized the order of every key. In fact, I was a lot quicker at typing than I was at writing by hand. I practiced, and practiced, and practiced tracing letters between the lines and cutting shapes. The difficulty and pain of gripping a pencil and scissors made me cry on a regular basis. With children's scissors, my occupational therapist helped me try several different methods of holding the scissors in my hand until it was far less painful, and a lot easier to operate.

Memories of equestrian therapy

Horses have always been my favorite animal. When our family doctor referred me to a horseback riding academy[1] specializing in equestrian therapy, I was willing to commit myself to the entire process. Equestrian therapy uses horseback riding for therapeutic purposes, to promote emotional growth and wellbeing in people with disabilities.

---

1   Canadian Association for Riders with Disabilities (CARD): a therapeutic riding center.

In February 2020, I emailed Seana Waldon, the Program Director at the Canadian Association for Riders with Disabilities (CARD), a few questions about equestrian therapy and she eagerly replied to the questions I sent her way. According to Seana, here's what you need to know about the horse's role in the equestrian therapy process:

> For those who underestimate the challenge to the horses, I ask how they might feel carrying a full backpack on one shoulder all day long (assuming they don't typically do this). If it is a particularly young person asking this question, I also remind them most therapy horses are mature adults, even seniors, and I ask them to consider the backpack scenario as if the person carrying the bag, was their grandmother.

For that exact reason, I never felt like I was in any danger. Every horse was carefully trained and monitored. This made it possible for the instructors to give students the therapy they deserve. The first time I rode a horse, a volunteer was by my side, and they kept me safe. I learned the basics with an experienced rider by my side. Eventually, the volunteer let me control the reins of the horse on my own. For the volunteer to finally let go of the horse, I had to earn my independence.

I was a little nervous at first about taking control of a powerful animal that doesn't like sudden movements, though the horse quickly proved me wrong through its patience and composure. In fact, my horse was so well trained that it could easily compensate for my lack of spatial awareness. When I was too close to somebody else's horse, the horse would stomp its feet and make a noise that sounded like a soft "purr." When I wasn't clear enough about the direction I wanted to go, the horse would either stop moving or move based on the direction I was moving my hands.

The horseback riding academy was also my first opportunity to meet people my age with disabilities. Some were in wheelchairs, and some had developmental disabilities. According to my mother, most of the horseback riding academy's students had more severe disabilities than I did. To me, the students were a friendly, approachable peer group. So, the severity of their disabilities was an afterthought. I was making friends and got invited to parties and sleepovers, and that made the entire process a lot more enjoyable.

Neither my family nor I were sure that my becoming an independent person was an achievable goal. CARD proved us all wrong. If I could control and manage a horse, maybe, just maybe, I could control and manage all other aspects of my life without help or assistance. Eventually, I got so good at horseback riding that one of my instructors taught me how to do dressage. Every weekend, we would practice the latest dressage routine. On a regular basis, my instructor enrolled me in dressage competitions at Toronto's Royal Winter Fair, along with horseback riding competitions in the Kitchener and Waterloo area.

Sometimes, I rode a beautiful white stallion named Misty; and sometimes, I rode a brown and white thoroughbred named Seamus. I had already emotionally bonded with them both, but grooming and feeding them on Saturday mornings before a competition helped deepen our shared sense of trust.

It took me years to realize this, but by deepening my bond with the horses, I was continuing my therapy process, enhancing my muscle strength and motor skills, and enhancing my confidence in my independence and self-worth. I loved spending time with the horses so much that I didn't even care if I won or lost my dressage competitions. It was a privilege to be able to ride these horses at all, and I always kept that in mind.

Other types of therapy I received

As part of my DCD therapy, my mom signed me up for everything from therapeutic gymnastics to ballet. At the time, they were just fun activities where I could pretend to be Ballerina Barbie, or an Olympic gymnast, but the more I read about the therapeutic benefits of both these activities, the more I understand my mom's motivations. Benefits include learning how to control your muscle movements (Richard, 2016), and that was something I struggled with back then; anything movement-based takes a lot of practice and time for dyspraxics to figure it out. Classes were conducted on a seasonal basis, and we received end-of-term report cards that outlined our progress.

If you did well on your report card, you could take a class in the next term at the next level of difficulty. Having other students working toward similar goals always motivated me to reach new levels of my personal best. To me, the most important part of all was the performances at the end of the term, because it always came with a feeling of accomplishment. Every performance was an opportunity to prove to our families that we were improving. Seeing my parents that happy and full of hope was a massive self-esteem boost. When mistakes were made, part of the therapy was starting with positive feedback, and then talking about how a child could improve upon their mistake next time. It was hard work, but the reward was the best part; my therapy activities always ended with long walks with our family pet, an English springer spaniel named Glory, and pizza for dinner.

A TV program that taught me spatial awareness 101

I still struggle with spatial concepts like how many blocks apart buildings are, and what makes something a shortcut; although my sense of space and time used to be a lot worse. In the early days of my diagnosis, I couldn't even read a clock and understand what time it was.

Surprisingly enough, what helped me learn how to tell time was a children's TV show. The year that I was diagnosed, *Big Comfy Couch* premiered on Canadian children's TV station YTV. It was a show that resembled an intense drug trip, and focused on Lunette the clown, her companion, a ragdoll named Molly, and a few other clowns who lived in her neighborhood. For me, the highlight was Lunette's clock stretch.

On a mat designed to look like a clock, she would move both her legs. All her movements resembled the movements and behavior of an analog clock. At the end of the stretch, she would wave and smile at the camera. I was five years old, and I laughed and smiled my way through it. This was the very first time that the concept of a clock in motion seemed fun and made sense to me. Then, I tuned into one episode after another. Both the clock stretch routine and the fictional world Lunette lived in interpreted space and time in an abstract fashion.

The show's abstract interpretation of the world made a lot more sense to me than the "real world." Just like me, Lunette and her friends tripped and fell, because they didn't understand the limitations of their environment. The more Lunette did her clock stretch skit, the more inaccessible concepts like clockwise and counterclockwise made sense to me.

Chapter 2

Early Years and Elementary School

How elementary schools and daycares handled my dyspraxia diagnosis

At school, my parents helped me get access to the school's special education department. Before getting a special education referral, I went through the rigorous process of being accessed by a committee of educators; all the educators that conducted my assessment were members of the identification, placement, and review committee (IPRC). I then got an individual education plan (IEP). The IEP is a mandatory document for students based in the Canadian province of Ontario who require special education. The IEP helps teachers figure out what changes to the curriculum are needed for students with disabilities to thrive at school.

Decades after it was first created, I finally read an electronic copy of my IPRC report, and that's when I realized that the person assessing me genuinely liked and cared about me. Clearly, this process was more than a job for the woman who wrote, organized, and conducted my assessment. When describing her interactions with me, words like "charming," "warm," and "delightful" were used. Since the IPRC mainly focused on what I can't do, her flattering words were a refreshing contrast. I realized that my memories of the IPRC testing process were slightly different than how everyone involved in this process saw it at the time. For so many years, I had felt nothing but anger about it.

I would have been less resentful if more time had been spent on talking me through the assessment process in between evaluations. Even though I was a tiny preschooler back then, I was a lot more self-aware than most adults thought. All the poking, prodding, and evaluating without explanation made me very upset, exhausted, and nervous. One test just kept leading to another. The whispered tones of the IPRC committee, and their tendency to always be scribbling notes in response to my words and actions, made me feel like a lab rat trapped in a maze.

When I got my first special education assessment, my biggest fear was permanent social isolation. I didn't know or understand how dyspraxia would affect me long term, so I assumed the worst. If this process was something that happened in my adulthood, I would at least have had plenty of unconditional peer support. The one thing that hasn't changed though is my relationship with my family; they have always loved and supported me unconditionally. Despite the support of my family, I always felt like I was hiding a small portion of myself from everyone else. At school, most of my peers knew I was under the careful guidance of the special education department. But since I did not yet know how to describe dyspraxia to other people, my peers didn't understand how or why I was getting special education support.

When I joined the special education "system," ADHD had a lot more awareness than dyspraxia. I was easily distracted, and this led to my teachers mislabeling my disability (Missiuna, Gaines, & Soucie, 2006). The main issue was the environment I was learning in, which had too much sensory stimulation to process, and too much pressure to reach someone else's idea of success.

Eventually, my mom had to intervene by showing up at the school to explain that my problem wasn't lack of focus, it was "too much focus." Social anxiety about not being able to articulate what I was going through led to comments on report cards about "not playing well with others" and "not participating in class." In settings like day camps and daycare, staff members expressed similar concerns.

The first time my parents dropped me off at a local daycare, I was quiet all afternoon. At the end of the workday my mother picked me up on her way home from work. I screamed the word "Mommy" and ran toward her. The people working there looked visibly shocked and didn't think that I could talk. This made my mother so angry that she transferred me to a different daycare.

After a really bad experience at daycare, blending in with the other children, and mimicking other people's idea of normal seemed like the most logical survival mechanism; this survival mechanism is often referred to as "masking" in the neurodiversity patient advocacy community.[1] Masking is often seen as a necessary survival mechanism in environments that have a negative perception of neurodiverse people's strengths and weaknesses. The very first time I started to mask my diagnosis, I learned that the joys of masking are short-lived, because the consequences aren't worth the effort.

I also didn't look disabled, so the adults that took care of me expected me to learn at the same pace as the other children. I got poor grades, and occasionally I got in trouble. Most of the authority figures in my life weren't sure how to handle a kid who couldn't learn at the same pace as everyone else.

Since I was diagnosed when I was still in kindergarten, I lacked the language, life experiences, and resources to self-advocate. So, I progressed at a slower rate than my peers with everything I was learning in school. I couldn't tie my shoelaces or ride a bike, something that my classmates did effortlessly; this made me feel excluded and isolated from my peers.

Although my diagnosis wasn't the only reason why I progressed in school at a slightly slower rate, it seemed like my

---

1   Patient advocates are people who live with a specific disability or chronic illness that advocate for people with a similar diagnosis. What sets them apart from parents, academics, and practitioners who don't have that diagnosis is their emphasis on lived experience.

greatest obstacle. Very few people understood the symptoms of my disability. Explaining it to other people was a frustrating endeavor. No matter what, dyspraxia would still manifest itself in my everyday life. Without a diagnosis, its setbacks would have no medical explanation. A medical explanation forces people to be more forgiving. For as long as I can remember, knowing exactly why I will face certain challenges has taken stress and uncertainty out of the equation.

The benefits and eccentricities of the Canadian alternative school system

In my first few years of school, I learned coping mechanisms through trial and a lot of error. My disability made me a target for my peer group, and even though I had some friends, I never felt like I fit in.

The greatest saving was my socially progressive parents. From a very young age, they took my perspective on the education I was receiving seriously. This made it very easy for me to speak up when something wasn't working for me. Back then, I attended Downtown Alternative School (DAS), one of the most progressive schools in Toronto. So, my school's way of doing things was a bit different to begin with.

When Esther Fine, a York University professor who teaches Education, asked me if I wanted to reflect on my experiences at DAS for the epilogue of her book, I eagerly provided my perspective. My brother was involved in her documentary on the same subject. So, I knew and trusted her.

The people who made the documentary talked to him twice: the first time was when he was a DAS student, and the second time was when he was a teenager. They wanted to document how the alternative school system affects people. Here's an abridged version of how I described my DAS experience:

> *At an early age, our teachers taught us how to handle conflict like mature adults. If a little girl was in tears in the classroom after recess, it was time for a peace circle. If someone wasn't sharing their toys like they promised, it was also time for a peace circle. If anyone had a problem, we'd work towards a solution together. It never involved violence, screaming, or name-calling. ... I blame DAS for making me a good friend, girlfriend, daughter, etc. If I ever have children, I hope their problems are never deemed unimportant. (Bascia, Fine, & Levine, 2017)*

When we did peacebuilding, aka "peace circles," we would stop what we were doing, sit in a circle, and listen to the point of view of everyone involved in a dispute. Then, we would compromise based on what triggered the argument in the first place. Since my school had an unorthodox approach to education, I was part of a community of kids whose parents felt like outcasts in their society. Most of my peers were the sons and daughters of performing arts professionals, musicians, artists, and intellectuals.

What made a really big difference was Judy, my kindergarten teacher. Judy wore colorful outfits with illustrations of birds and various other animals, had a short, frizzy hairdo, and a presence that resembled a children's TV presenter. This made her instantly approachable to all children who spent time in her classroom. She genuinely cared about her students. Despite all that, she wasn't a pushover. Judy was my most powerful advocate at a difficult stage of my life where I didn't feel in control of anything. If members of the DAS community treated me poorly, she would be there to help. Only my mother rivaled Judy's high level of dedication to creating a supportive environment. When I was in school, my mother was the type of parent who wasn't afraid to show up at school and tell off everyone and anyone who upset me.

When I was diagnosed with dyspraxia, my mother was an undeserving target of blame. Some members of the older generation of my family blamed my mom for things I couldn't do because of my neurodiverse characteristics. It turns out my elders were simply a product of the era they grew up in. My grandparents grew up at a time when autism and other types of neurodevelopmental disorders were portrayed in books, studies, and popular culture as the product of bad parenting (Silberman, 2016). Instead of assuming that my elders were right, the need to constantly prove them wrong made my mom a stronger advocate.

In Judy's classroom, I got a lot of support from a student teacher who taught me how to read. She also helped me develop fine and gross motor skills. My student teacher provided one-on-one tutoring. The tutoring process stopped when I developed a basic understanding of words and could pick up a pencil and write or draw something. Meanwhile, I was remembering complex stories in extreme detail. Sounds of letters, and the alphabet confused me. When I wrote something by hand, the spelling and construction of words wouldn't match how the actual words looked in my head.

Despite all those challenges, I had the vocabulary of someone a lot older than me. Once my teachers realized this, I was a lot better off. My love of words started to become a reward rather than a source of frustration. My parents read stories to me every night, and the more they read stories to me, the more my ability to read and write improved.

Dealing with a teacher who refused to accommodate me

By the end of my kindergarten year I moved on to the first year of primary school. In grade 1, my teacher wasn't as sympathetic or accommodating as Judy. My teacher didn't let me write with a typewriter, use a calculator for complex math equations, or have extra time outside of the classroom for tests.

The three most important advocates in my life at the time— Judy and my parents—did everything that they could to get me proper accommodations. Eventually, they came up with a suitable compromise. At school, I would practice my handwriting and basic math independently with Judy and be graded based on my progress. All other activities I would do in the slightly less accommodating teacher's classroom.

Thanks to Judy and my parents' valiant efforts and hard work, I passed my first year of primary school at the same pace as my peers.

How unconventional learning made a huge difference

When I progressed to year two and three of primary school, Darin became my teacher. Coincidentally enough he was also the teacher who had given my brother permission to leave his class every two hours to participate in my brushing therapy. Darin looked exactly like David Bowie in the 1990s, because they both wore round glasses and floral, collared shirts.

On the first day of school, it was clear that Darin had done his homework. He knew about my disability and knew exactly how to accommodate me properly. This put my parents at ease, who had gone through so much to accommodate the challenges of my disability.

All of Darin's classes were fun and educational. On a regular basis, he brought all sorts of things to class, everything from snakes to tortoises. Unlike the teacher I had in my first year of primary school, Darin had a very unconventional approach to teaching. He would teach students indoors and outdoors, while including child-friendly pop culture references in classroom discussions. This approach was perfect for me, because it was at a slower pace and not nearly as strict as my grade 1 classroom environment.

The trouble with bullying: why I left DAS in my fourth year of primary school

In my third year of primary school, I learned that peace circles can't correct the behavior of someone who feels no remorse or regrets. DAS only offers kindergarten to grade 6 classes. So, my brother had to transfer to Parkdale Collegiate for grades 7 and 8. Suddenly, the bigger, stronger, older brother who protected me from harm wasn't a DAS student. Since I wasn't as well protected as I once was, I experienced my first bully. My struggles learning at the same pace as the other students made me a target for the girl that everyone was afraid of.

On a regular basis, the bully teased me, and pointed out my dyspraxia-induced flaws, such as how I walked, talked, and processed verbal instructions. This was such a constant part of my life at school that I stopped connecting on a social level with my peers. Stories of fairies and magical creatures were my refuge; books were my new best friends.

When I didn't feel like my learning environment was safe enough, I spoke to an adult I trusted. All that adult really did was point out why my bully's behavior was bad. This made the teasing worse. When nothing happened, this triggered a peace circle.

In the peace circle, one of my teachers was the moderator. Then my peers quietly sat in a circle, as the bully and I both described our side of the story. Unsurprisingly enough, the bully felt great about everything that had happened. Meanwhile, I felt terrible about their behavior. This made it impossible for us to resolve our differences. No one did anything about it and this whole thing got forgotten about. The bullying continued, while I worked hard to pass every test and class project.

Then, I told my parents that I wanted to switch to a different school. Without my having to explain why it was necessary, they took my requests seriously and recommended a school on the Toronto Islands. Before transferring me to a new school, we took the ferry and got a tour of the facilities. One year later,

I transferred to the Island Public Natural Science School, and the bully was no longer my problem.

Adjusting to a new school

Within my first few months of being an Island Public Natural Science School student, I learned that going to school on the Toronto Islands had its benefits. Although the best part of it all was how it changed the mentality of the average student. Teachers, artists, and puppeteers live there. What I admired the most about the residents is their ability to never stop fighting for what they believe in. If they didn't like what was going on in local politics, they organized petitions and protests. If necessary, they would also talk to the media about their concerns. Anything that made you different was celebrated, and Toronto Island residents approached things they didn't understand with curiosity rather than fear.

Half of the students were commuting via ferry every day, and half of us were children of the Toronto Islands full-time residents. At the time, one of my closest friends was a Toronto Islands resident who lived with her family on a boat that was permanently docked on Ward's Island.[2]

Every day, our teachers combined traditional classroom teaching with hands-on experiences. We learned through a mixture of nature, art, and culture that the City of Toronto and the Toronto Islands had to offer. Going outside and learning about the wildlife that lived on the islands was just another day at school.

On the islands, retired police horses wandered around the playground. They were clever creatures who snatched food out of the hands of schoolchildren. The best interruption of all was Java, the principal's chocolate Labrador retriever. Every day, Java

---

2   Ward's Island is where the majority of the Toronto Islands residents live. It is one of a few islands connected to the Toronto Islands.

would show up in our classrooms and patrol the hallways. He was friendly, patient, curious, and would always put a smile on everyone's faces. In fact, he wouldn't leave until he got enough attention. If a student had anything on their hands, their hands were licked clean. Then Java would either go to the next class-room or have a quick nap in the principal's office.

At Island Public Natural Science School, I got good grades and I was fitting in a lot better than I had at my previous school, and I was a lot happier for that exact reason. Since it was a small school, my teachers offered one-on-one support when something was difficult.

One time, because of a doctor's appointment, I came to school late. When I finally made it to the island portion of the ferry docks, the school bus driver, Karl, drove me to school. I don't remember how it came up, but I mentioned I was struggling with learning how to multiply things by the number 9. Karl chimed in and repeated the nine times tables in order until the bus arrived at its destination. Just like everything else in my life at that point, logical patterns based on memorizing things in order stuck in my head better than anything else. Karl reminded me to memorize my times tables in numerical order so that a pattern would stick in my brain. When I thought of "1 times 9," followed by "9 times 9," the answers to the equations got scrambled in my brain. When I thought of the answer to "1 times 9," followed by the answer to "2 times 9" I had the answers memorized.

Falling in love (with running and racing)
I fondly remember, and often talk about coach Burt, because he was my gym teacher who convinced me to join the school's cross-country team. Burt was such a huge influence that I wrote a story about him years later in a writers' group writing exercise:

I remember the first time I hit the track. I ran faster, and faster, and felt freer, and freer. Everyone was cheering, then I reached the finish line. Burt was smiling, but I never knew smiling was his style. Every time I ran, my time got better. Burt seemed happier; the team seemed happier. I learned how to pace myself and I learned how to stretch my muscles so that I wouldn't hurt myself. "No, I can't" turned to "yes I can." Then, race day happened, and I didn't know how to win, but Burt's smile suggested otherwise. "Bang" went the start gun. Several competitors were ahead of me, and so many people were cheering that I couldn't hear what they were saying. I saw Burt's smile at the corner of my eye and the urge to just keep moving strengthened. The race started with a bang and ended with the strongest and fastest pace I had ever done. At the finish line, everyone hugged. Then we found out that our team was the first 30 people to reach the finish line. Moments later, Burt joined the celebration.

Clearly, Burt saw me as a runner with a lot of potential, and that meant a lot to me at the time. With time and practice, I got stronger, faster, and more in control of my own body. It wasn't easy to have Burt as a coach, but his approach was effective. He pushed all his student athletes beyond the limits of how fast or for how long they thought they could run. He also taught us how to recognize the limits of what we can do and never put our health in danger.

With his authoritative, deep voice, and tall, skinny, muscular stature, he towered over and commanded his students. When he told his students that running was about a lot more than just running, everyone listened. Although Burt was serious and intense most of the time, he had a huge heart and a kind soul.

Switching schools after learning to fit in

When I was an Island School student, I felt like I had a chance at a "normal" life for the very first time, but the Island School only goes up to grade 6. On my final day of being an island school student, I walked away from the ferry docks, crying in my father's arms. The sun was shining, and it was a beautiful day, but I had to say goodbye to all my friends.

I always hated change when I was only just starting to feel comfortable. I don't feel comfortable all that easily because I never really know if I am in an environment where masking the key characteristics of my disability and keeping my symptoms to myself is necessary. I can charm people, but I can't fake the feeling of warm summer breeze where people accept the bad parts as well.

Chapter 3

Getting My Period and Other Pre-Teen Milestones

By age 12, I was officially registered for King Edward Public school, where students were expected to be on surname terms with their teachers. This was the very first time that I was expected to call my teacher by their last name, and having to address everyone older than me as "Ms." or "Mr." was an overdue lesson in respecting my elders. It was also an extremely structured environment—something that I desperately needed. If you asked me for my opinion when I was 12, I probably would have told you about how strict it felt in comparison to my socially progressive upbringing and the schools I had attended up till then.

In my first few months at the new school, I got my first period, and hormones clouded my judgment. Everything was changing inside me, and dyspraxia could not keep up with all these changes. Puberty was a phase where all the changes in my body made my dyspraxia symptoms a hundred times worse. All the coping mechanisms that I had learned in my childhood didn't make sense anymore, and other people's expectations were brand new. I had to watch out for menstrual blood on my clothes and not talk about periods, but I could barely eat or walk around without making a huge mess.

I also had to sit in a chair, and only bend my arms and legs in certain ways to be "lady-like." Body hair grew in unflattering places, and everyone wanted me to go to my first nail salon.

My first nail salon was treated like a rite of passage, but I resented it. The music was too loud, and the instructions made no sense. Feisty Asian ladies barked instructions at me, and the more I looked at them confused, the more their eyes rolled. The feeling of nail polish being applied to my skin made me feel as uncomfortable and irritated as I had imagined it would.

With an unsteady hand and a lack of interest in ever returning to a nail salon, nail polish became a rare event. I only wore nail polish when other people wanted to "do my nails." Sometimes, I still paint my own nails, but my hands always shake, and the polish is always a sloppy mess on both the table and my fingers. Not to mention the smell, a powerful chemical smell that I genuinely hate. So, it's something I only do when there's a special event.

Soon after my first nail salon experience, I had my first shaving experience when a family member shamed me for the hair under my arms and on my legs. Quietly in my parents' bathroom I locked the door and tried out a razor I had found in my mom's cosmetics drawer. Then I rubbed the razor against my skin. It was extremely painful, I cried a bit, and I drew some blood, but it did the job. Next time the hair grew back, I applied soap and warm water to my skin, and it didn't hurt or draw blood.

Confronting everyone else's expectations about womanhood

Other people's expectations about the person I was "supposed to be" were so unrealistic that I immersed myself in *Harry Potter*, *Series of Unfortunate Events*, and *Chronicles of Narnia* novels instead. These books were an enormous source of comfort for me because the protagonists were relatable people who also struggled to fit in, but who were eventually (spoiler alert) welcomed with open arms in mythical worlds where their identity was an advantage. As I read these books, I daydreamed about the day when someone, somewhere would accept me for who I am.

I'm biologically a woman, but many of the expectations that

came with "being a woman" made no sense to me. There were too many knots to tie, buttons to maneuver, and clasps to navigate. Whenever I got dressed, the buttons and complex knots of women's clothing were a source of frustration. I would put my clothes on in such a wonky fashion that I moved around stiffly for the rest of the day.

Trading in my clasp- and button-heavy clothes for button- and knot-free alternatives was a start, but every day, it took multiple tries for my clothes to not be inside out and backwards. Getting dressed was a lot less frustrating when I hyper-focused on the process of putting my clothes on. This made it possible for me to focus on the details of the clothing, and not lose track of what I did two seconds ago.

When I was a pre-teen girl, I was always late for something, hyper-focusing when you're in a hurry is impossible. To work around this challenge, I allowed a lot more time to get dressed in the morning and get up earlier, but I'm not a morning person. I have always struggled with turning off my hyperactive brain at night. Eventually, I fixed that problem once getting to bed and waking at a certain time became a routine; this minor adjustment was totally worth it for not having to walk around all day with the knowledge that my clothes were on backwards, and all my zippers and buttons were wonky.

Sensory sensitivity has also made wearing clothes so much more complicated. My pre-teen years were a time when I learned the hard way which fabrics irritated me to the point of all-day distraction, and which fabrics were tolerable. I learned what I can tolerate through a painful trial-and-error process, but this process had to be balanced out with feeling good in what I'm wearing. Both these factors rarely matched up perfectly.

At that age, I had so much left to learn about what being a woman means, but the idea of womanhood a lot of us are exposed to is someone's attempt at trying to sell something anyways.

Personal grooming: Hair and makeup

Girls my age wore makeup, and I couldn't keep makeup brushes or accessories still in my hand. Everyone assumed that I was never going to learn how to apply makeup. So, none of the women in my life bothered to teach me. I also lacked the motor skills and spatial awareness to properly apply lipstick, mascara, and eyeliner, although I was determined to learn, because not understanding makeup made me a bit of an outcast. I hated feeling like an outcast. So, I bought makeup at a local drugstore and tried to practice using makeup tools on my own.

I was so unsure about what I was doing that I bought cheap drugstore makeup that falls apart easily. I tried to apply makeup in the bathroom mirror at home, but I looked like a carnival clown. So, I finally asked for help from my family and told everyone else that I applied the makeup on my own. I couldn't hide the fact that other people were applying my makeup for me forever, because makeup was the office water cooler of female friendships. It was what you did if you wanted to spread gossip or bond with other women.

At my local makeup store, I worked up the courage to ask the people working in the cosmetics department for help. It took two women who reminded me of my mom, and one gender-ambiguous person to finally understand how this process works. All the people I spoke to were happy to walk me through the makeup application process until I could hold makeup in my hands without smearing it all over my face. Every day, I practiced in the mirror everything that the friendly people in the cosmetics department had taught me.

The more I practiced, the more I learned that hyper-focusing and tuning out all other forms of background noise steadied my chronically unsteady hands, while helping me put makeup on in a straight line. My local cosmetics store was left with a feeling of accomplishment, but my brother did not approve.

My sudden interest in makeup and how I looked triggered a lot of arguments between my brother and me. My brother believed that my obsession with makeup did me more harm than good, and I think that he was right all along, but it took me so many years to realize that.

Nowadays the only makeup that I wear is my "ruby-red," a red shade of lipstick that I feel good in. At this point, I have put my ruby-red on my mouth so many times that applying it is second nature to me.

Learning how to brush and take care of my hair had similar challenges. I tried to wear my hair long, but I would often forget to brush it, and my hair would end up in painful knots. I spent a large chunk of my pre-teen years with short hair, but then a photographer at a school picture day mistook me for a guy.

The "photographer incident" upset me so much that I grew out my hair long and couldn't stand having it short until my mid-20s. With a bit of practice, I got pretty good at tying my hair in a ponytail. Hairbands and clips also solved the chronic issues with forgetting to brush my hair. Clips, hairbands, and ponytails were a good visual reminder that signified that yes... I had remembered to brush my hair that day! Just like with showering and makeup, I had to follow consistent patterns and hyper-focus for my unsteady hands and poor short-term memory not to completely fail me.

The challenges of learning at a fast pace

I loved language, and I was keen and eager to learn something new, but in the Extended French Program, I struggled. My Extended French provided a large class size and a rapid pace, and I couldn't keep up. Then, I made friends with French Immersion students. My French Immersion friends were a huge help because they had been immersed in the French language since primary school.

My most influential savior, though, was a special education teacher named Mr. D. Mr. D took the information he learned while reading my IEP and helped me organize school and life.

After talking to me, he picked up on my feelings of shame about my disability. Together, we worked on my poor organization and time-management skills. Mr. D is the reason why I still use Post-it Notes, track important days and events in a mixture of notebooks and electronic calendar reminders, and have a whiteboard that tracks new clients, projects, and events.

Mr. D and I worked on other important stuff as well, like finding the language and vocabulary to talk about my strengths and weaknesses. Reflecting on my strengths and weaknesses in a journal-writing format helped me go from not being able to describe how others can help to being able to find the words I needed to say to the adults in my life:

> I have dyspraxia. Here are the challenges it creates. I'm great at the following, and I struggle with the following tasks...

How I made friends with my bullies

When other people made me feel isolated and alone, I often found solace in my favorite books instead of people for a while. Mr. D helped me overcome my tendency to bottle up my dissatisfaction about how others were treating me. This important event happened soon after he saw the school bully knock my pencil case out of my hand and demanded that I pick it up. When my hand was on the ground, the bully stomped her foot against my hand as her friend laughed. Instead of sticking up for myself I passively accepted her behavior.

When the bullies left, Mr. D snuck up on me and told me that he wanted a word with me. I thought I was in trouble, but what he said to me made me realize that I had done nothing wrong: "I saw what happened just now. Are those girls...bothering you?"

I nodded my head and then there was a long silence. Then, I silently looked at Mr. D for a while, terrified to speak up as he said to me: "You shouldn't let people treat you like that. Next time they do that, don't listen to them, and ask them to pick up your pencil case instead. Do not be afraid. They're not as scary as they seem."

The next time the bully knocked something out of my hands, I asked her to pick it up and told her to stop being so mean to people. She reacted with anger as she told me that she was going to "kick my ass" if I didn't pick up my pencil case. I responded with stories about my big, strong, elder brother who is going to join the army next year. I exaggerated how big and strong he is, but that comment made her go silent. After that silence, I said, "How about you pick this up instead and say sorry." And she did.

She didn't bother me again after that day. A week later I found the school bully's friend in the bathroom, looking anxious and embarrassed. There was a red stain on her clothing, and she immediately asked me if I had any tampons or pads. Quietly, I handed a maxi pad to her, and she admitted this was her first period. From the other side of the door, I gave her instructions on how pads work, and reassured her that everything was going to be alright. We never spoke of this incident again.

By my final month of grade 8, my former bully and I had overcome our differences and managed to work together. Our teachers asked us to memorize and perform *Anansi the Spider* in front of a crowd of kindergarten students. The children smiled and laughed their way through the performance.

By then, I was doing better than I ever had at school. I passed grade 8 because more creative outlets were available than ever before. Finally, I had a safe environment where I could explore my love of writing.

Chapter 4

Secondary School and Preparing for University

At the end of grade 8, I had to think about high school: the next milestone.[1] My first choice was Rosedale School of the Arts. So I applied for its rigorous audition process. By then, my brother was 16 years old and was a member of the local Military Reservist regiment, so he knew a thing or two about what a structured environment can do for a person. He wanted to keep me away from a culture of drugs and relaxed rules about student behavior. That year, a lot of our former DAS peers entered the art school system; all of them surrendered to peer pressure and joined a culture of teen sex, drugs, and parties. My brother understood me better than I can understand myself, and he wanted to make sure I was university-bound. Since I've always looked up to my brother, it took minimal effort for him to change my mind.

My brother is the main reason why I went to Harbord Collegiate Institute, which has a high university acceptance rate. I wanted to dedicate my adulthood to writing, and I was smart enough to know that I needed to get into university for writing to be a realistic career choice.

When I became a student at Harbord, I learned that their high

---

1   In Ontario, the term "secondary school" refers to grades 9–12. The words "secondary school" and "high school" are used interchangeably in this context. Grades 1–8 are known as "elementary" (primary).

university acceptance rate was more than an admission pamphlet talking point. In fact, it was the opposite of the hippy, relaxed "we're all friends here" alternative school system I experienced in my childhood. The rules were strict, and the curriculum was based on the teachers' genuine interest in preparing students for post-secondary education.

With every course you took, you were immediately placed into a bubble of Academic (university-prep) or Applied (college-prep). By age 14, I knew that I wanted to go to university, but I only excelled at English, Arts, and Humanities. I made the mistake of picking Academic for most areas, except my weakest subjects (Science and Math). Some classes, such as Geography, were harder than I assumed.

The consequences of not understanding maps and distance

Often, the expectations were so high in my Geography class that I would leave class in tears. It didn't help that the Geography teacher would lock you out of the class if you were even a minute late for class. Back then my spatial awareness and my awareness of how much time it takes to get from point A to point B were a lot worse.

I had far less technology and fewer coping methods than I do now. I went to secondary school pre-smartphones and Google Maps wasn't as widely available as it is now. Pre-smartphones, my friends and family had to tell me how much time it takes to get from one location to the other and write down verbal instructions. For me to understand where I was going, words like "turn right at this street" did nothing but confuse me. Friends and family had to rely on landmarks for me to understand. However, they didn't always have the time or patience to do that.

My punctuality problem was a lack of spatial awareness issue rather than something I did because I didn't care. My route from home to school changed constantly based on which family member was available. So, I never got the chance to memorize a route or find out what bus I had to take at what time to be on time.

Multiple times a week, I started off my Geography class morning by being locked out of the classroom for 15–20 minutes and being yelled at "Because punctuality is important!" One day, I was finally early, and that was only because I at last had a photographic memory of my route from home to school memorized. The punishment for being late all the time wasn't worth it in the end because the course material was extremely difficult.

Drawing maps requires spatial awareness, and that's what we did in class most of the time. Although I couldn't just drop the class since it was a requirement for graduation. No matter how hard I concentrated or practiced, my knowledge of where things were didn't translate into a legible map. I failed every test and assignment, and the teacher refused to blame my failure on anything else besides not listening or caring.

Eventually, I had to convince my brother to help me with my final assignment. In that assignment, I had to draw a map of Canada. I told my brother where everything was supposed to go on the map, and he drew the map based on my instructions. Clearly, it worked because I passed Geography, and never had to worry about it again.

Meanwhile, I was the star pupil of every English class that I took. I felt bored and not challenged enough in my English classes until my final year of secondary school. In this final year, my English teacher was such a huge fan of my writing that he was my harshest and most difficult-to-please critic, although I didn't figure that out until the last day of school when he told me I was one of the best writers he'd ever taught.

What did special education look like in secondary school?

From the very beginning of secondary school, my accommodations were a continuation of what I received soon after I started primary school. Every test was taken in an alternate environment, Harbord's resource room, the onsite room for students who need special education support, and extra time for tests. Both these accommodations did wonders for my sensory issues. It's extremely difficult for me to produce decent work in noisy environments where you're under a tremendous amount of pressure.

Sometimes, I could also request extra time for assignments since I get very overwhelmed when I'm overloaded with stuff to do, which can damage the quality of the work I produce. Although I only seemed to need that accommodation in the subjects I found difficult.

Every time I went up a grade level, the Special Education Department loosened its support and hand-holding a little bit more. There was always a lot of paperwork involved in this process, and every teacher would get a form signed by the Special Education Department that disclosed my accommodation requirements. From age 14–15, the special education teachers would come to my classes, and make sure that my accommodations were taken seriously. By the time I was age 16, they would only participate in the process if I asked for their help.

Meanwhile, my special education teachers were teaching me useful life skills, such as managing my time, figuring out what points are important when reading notes or textbooks, and memorizing important facts. When I was 17 years old, the Special Education Department helped me apply for university. When my acceptance letters arrived, they helped me figure out what I wanted to major in.

At that point, my English springer spaniel, Glory, was old, frail, and slowly dying. Suddenly Glory couldn't move or eat. My parents had to take her to the vet and have her put down in the most humane way possible. As I said goodbye to her for the very last time, I gave her just as much love and compassion as she had given me since I was a small child. I hugged her, kissed her, petted her gently, and told her I loved her. Time temporarily seemed a lot slower as an important sliver of my childhood became a pleasant memory.

Occasionally, Glory still appears in my dreams and offers support at the moments when I'm stressed out about something. Unconditionally, she offered love and support, something I needed so badly in the early years of living with dyspraxia.

Choosing a dyspraxia-friendly university

Soon after Glory's death, I had to figure out where I wanted to go to university. At first, I thought I was going to go to the University of Windsor for English Literature and Creative Writing. I had heard nothing but good things about their writing program but had never been to Windsor. Although my family didn't seem to like the idea of my going to Windsor, my mom wanted to support my choices with an open mind.

For my mom, this involved booking train tickets to Windsor, and doing a campus tour. When we visited the campus, it had a cold, industrial look. It was also massive, and it was way too high stimulus for me. I could only take its noisy atmosphere in small doses. In high-stimuli environments, my dyspraxic brain processes verbal instructions and the limitations of my environment extremely slowly. To process my environment at an average rate, I must focus extremely hard, and that drains my energy.

Then there was the City of Windsor, which had the same smoggy, metallic, factory-like vibe. This was a huge deal-breaker due to my sensory processing issues. My dyspraxia is a lot more severe when I'm experiencing sounds or textures I have an above-average level of sensitivity towards. Breathing the city's polluted air gave me severe headaches, and I wanted to get back on that train as soon as possible.

The City of Windsor's energy, look, and feel also didn't appeal to me. I was still so young, and I was only just starting to understand how dyspraxia affects my life. What I immediately realized was that I needed access to familiar doctors and resources. I still didn't know if I could thrive in a university environment and didn't know what to expect. I could have waited a year or two and gained more life experiences, but I didn't want to wait. Good grades triggered early acceptance and bursaries from multiple universities. The universities that I applied to wanted me to enroll as soon as possible.

After taking Windsor off my list, I narrowed down my choices to two York University programs. This made it possible for me to have easy access to local resources, programs, and medical professionals. The main campus, the Keele Campus, failed to pique my interest though—its size was just as overwhelming as the University of Windsor. But then I went to an open house at the university's Glendon Campus and fell in love with its peace and tranquility.

The best part of Glendon was its classroom sizes and community, which were small and friendly. This created an environment where I could de-stress in a landscape filled with trees, and a park with its own walking path. It was also a shuttle ride away from the Keele Campus, where all the good writing classes were. As a student, I could ride that shuttle for free. Then, there were the on-campus activities, which immediately got my attention. I wanted to join *Pro Tem*, the campus newspaper, after I found an issue of *Pro Tem* at the entrance. Although what really sealed the deal for me was the theater community. I immediately fell in love with Glendon Theatre's small but well-equipped black box theater.

The only real issue I had with Glendon was the bilingual requirement; I had to take a certain number of French classes. Once I thought it over a bit, I remembered my days of successfully surviving King Edward Public School's Extended French program. I made it work once before, so I figured this was a hurdle I could overcome.

After the open house, I went online and accepted my offer from York University Glendon Campus' Drama Studies program. As soon as I was able to register for classes, I also signed up for some first-year English Literature classes. I wanted to switch to a double major in my second year.

For me, the transition from having access to a community of adults who are trained to deal with adolescents with disabilities, to being treated like an adult who must advocate for my own needs happened too quickly. When I was in secondary school, I didn't ask my special education teachers enough questions about how they advocate for their students. This was my biggest regret of all and made the transition into the post-secondary education system difficult.

According to the Dyspraxia Foundation's *Dyspraxia in the Workplace* pamphlet, dyspraxics are your best resource for figuring out how you can help them (Dyspraxia Foundation, 2016). Back then, I knew what that looked like in my childhood, but didn't know what that looked in my adulthood. So, I went from prom night, my final exams, and my graduation ceremony to my first year of university without proper resources or support.

Chapter 5

How the University System Handles Dyspraxia

When university started, I was informed that getting proper accommodations was my responsibility. Since I have an October birthday, I was 17 years old, and didn't turn 18 until my second month of university. Despite that, the university administration was already treating me like an adult. So, no one was holding my hand and telling me what I should be doing.

Although I was still in Toronto, I decided to give living on campus a try. When I did my on-campus residence application, disclosing my disability helped me avoid the stress of getting a roommate. I ended up in the women-only section of Wood Residence. This was a lonely choice that put me on a floor filled with women who had values and interests that were completely different than my own. The quieter ones either had English as a second language or were extremely religious. The older ones were only interested in parties and boyfriends. The drama club was the first place on campus where I met people I could relate to.

Since I was so young, the first few months had their own challenges. I was a lot more on my own than I ever had been. As great as my new-found independence was, I still wasn't well informed enough about my disability to make the right choices. Suddenly, I was my own advocate, and I was making a horrible job of it. Then, Gramps Norm died, a grandparent whom I had always looked up to. His death was so hard on me that I socially isolated myself from a peer group that was only just getting to know me.

My biggest mistake of all, though, was my choice to pretend that my disability didn't exist. I didn't tell my teachers, peers, or university administrators. This made my first two years unnecessarily complicated. My one source of comfort was my diary-writing habit, which helped me articulate what I was going through. A diary entry from my second year of university perfectly articulated the therapeutic role of diary writing at the time:

> I'm happy to have this routine back in my life again. I've kept a diary since I was 12 years old, and for some unexplainable reason I stopped keeping a diary this year. I found it helpful (I guess) because I could vent in a way. I didn't feel like I could talk openly and transparently about what I was thinking or feeling without fear of judgement.[1]

In my second year of university, I had reapplied for the room I'd lived in the previous year without considering my options, although I only lived there part-time. Since I was a 19-year-old kid who had reached the local legal drinking age that year, this was an excellent decision. Back then, I was drinking heavily at college parties to cope with social anxiety. My disability was a secret that I was failing to disclose to students, staff, and teachers and my social anxiety had never been higher.

I was afraid of what others would think of my dyspraxia and its symptoms, and I thought that pretending not to have a disability was the only solution. For the first time in my life, nothing was being done about my need for proper accommodations.

---

1   Diary entry from May 26th, 2010.

Suddenly, everyone was imposing high social and academic standards on me, and I didn't know how to ask for help.

The more I wrote in my diary, the more I found specific examples of what I was and wasn't finding difficult about all the different ways it showed up in my personal life:

> Nothing is more special for me than being able to write something out. People say that when I write stuff out it's pretty... clear. If I ever can't express something, people should just make me write stuff out. It makes me feel so complete and whole.[2]

What saved me the most were my essays, which I could do in the comfort of my own home. The essays gave me decent grades, which wasn't a huge surprise. My writing abilities got me into college, but I can never process or articulate what I'm thinking or feeling under pressure.

How I learned to stop ignoring my disability

When I was in my third year of university, I moved back in with my parents; I needed more help than ever with the complexities of keeping my disability a secret, having tried to manage it on my own for far too long. Being around family was the only way I was going to learn how to self-advocate. They had so many years of practice advocating on my behalf anyways. Eventually, I mentioned my disability to some of my drama club friends through vague statements about what I can't do.

The breaking point for me, however, was a few presentations I didn't practice for well enough; pretending not to be disabled had backfired, and that was the very first time I realized something:

---

2   Diary entry from March 3rd, 2011.

> *So, tomorrow's the big presentation day and I'm especially terrified. Taking this on has proved to be quite tough with everything else I have going on. Although I've probably got as much going on as everyone else, a big part of living your life with a disability is that no matter what you must work harder than everyone else to move at their pace. So, the projects at school have proved to be more than I can handle, and I didn't learn that until it was too late.*[3]

Luckily, by then, I was part of a peer group that was unconditionally supportive:

> *So, my final presentation for Baroque (theatre) class ended with a bang so I guess it went okay. Things were just what I had full faith in: that everything would turn out okay, because everyone would step in and support each other.*[4]

But my supportive peer group wasn't present in every course that I took. Sometimes, I had to adapt to new environments, and that was extremely challenging. A great example of this was when I took some summer classes at York University's Keele Campus, an environment I spent very little time in:

> *Taking classes at Keele (campus) feels like starting all over, as if suddenly I'm going back to first year (university) again. Even though that's not literally the case, it's psychologically the case. What I notice is that I'm always exhausted by the end,*

---

3   Diary entry from November 27th, 2012.
4   Diary entry from November 28th, 2012.

> *because I'm always trying hard with people, and none of them*
> *are people I've established an emotional relationship with. So,*
> *it's exhausting. I'm in this place I have very little familiarity with,*
> *and it's taking a long time to get a sense of grounding there. I*
> *blame the fact that the longest period I've spent at Keele was*
> *a couple of hours to go to class.*[5]

The key word, in this case is definitely "grounding." It's normal to have an awkward adjustment period in any new environment, but my disability made this process happen at a slower rate. On a social level, it happened when I met someone new; I wondered if they would accept me for who I am. Every week I'd get lost on my way to class.

Eventually I memorized nearby landmarks, but I didn't familiarize myself with Keele Campus fast enough. Then, there was the learning process, which had mixed results. Due to the campus' vast size, things got difficult when I had to adjust to large class sizes. I can't focus or process information in large lecture halls, especially in exam environments with large groups of people. Sometimes I would fail, even if I knew the answer.

The biggest game changer of all was having access to Facebook in its early years. In fact, I started university in 2009, when the number of people using Facebook was rapidly growing.

When I searched for dyspraxia on Facebook, I found two groups, run by not-for-profit organizations specializing in dyspraxia awareness and advocacy. One was U.K.-based, and one was based in the U.S., but both were equally valuable. Both groups were an open forum where people could get their dyspraxia-related questions and concerns answered. Eventually, I found the website of the people who ran these groups. Both websites offered accessible dyspraxia definitions and resources.

---

5   Diary entry from May 17th, 2012.

Yet they used medical lingo that you need a medical degree to understand. So, I had to find my own explanations.

I went to university when social media was beginning to explode in popularity. This created a positive platform for me to slowly embrace my disability as a key part of my identity. Online movements like the Cripple Movement (see Chapter 9) helped me proudly tell everyone that I have a disability. This was a big deal for me, because I was ashamed of my dyspraxia, and avoided it for way too long.

The final two years of university

As a Glendon student, what really held me back was Glendon's bilingual requirement. Glendon students must take a certain number of French language courses, or courses in French (one, not both of those things). At first, I got passing grades on every French course. Then I found myself in an advanced-level French class.

Unfortunately, the issue was my instructor, not the subject matter. Up until then, the patience and accommodating nature of my teachers was a lifesaver. In the Advanced French class, the instructor had an indifferent and bitter perspective on her students' problems. When I asked for specific accommodations, she rolled her eyes and didn't take me seriously. Instead, I got accused of not paying attention in class. No matter how hard I worked, I couldn't get anything besides a failing grade on course material.

The last straw for me though was when I was in a play on campus, and my instructor wouldn't let me miss a class to go to the final rehearsal. Despite my French teacher's lack of approval, I went to the rehearsal anyways. To avoid confrontation, I dropped her class online.

Yet I still had to take something that counted toward my French requirement. After asking around a bit, I found out that you can get the French requirement in two semesters.

The alternative was two computer courses, focusing on Excel spreadsheets and HTML. Both courses were taught in Franglais (a mix of French and English).

First, I took an extremely difficult Excel spreadsheet course that covered techniques that were more advanced than the spreadsheets used in most office environments. Then, there was the size of the class. I can't process information in large classrooms. Glendon is known for its small class sizes, but the computer classes are the size of the average university lecture hall. What saved me was my final assignment, which I could do from home at my own pace. In the end, the final assignment led to a good enough grade to pass the class and move on to part two, the HTML class.

On the first day of the HTML class, it was more people and a lot more background noise than I could handle. A paralyzing feeling of social anxiety made me quietly sneak out the back door and drop out of the class. I was hyperventilating so badly that I had to retreat somewhere quieter to be able to breathe again. Although I had completed all the required classes for my major stress-free, I couldn't graduate. So, I decided to apply for an additional, part-time semester.

In my part-time semester my grades went way up. I had to drop a theater course that didn't suit me too well, but dropping that course had no actual consequences. I was juggling a small course load, along with a paid internship at a local theater company. I learned so many practical skills. When I was ready to graduate, I had a great deal of confidence about what I could do.

For instance, my final HTML class assignment was a practice round for something I wanted to do when I graduated: create and publish my own consulting site. I was so driven by my own ambition that I aced the final assignment. My final assignment became the template for the copy and layout of my content creation and strategy business's website.

PART II

INTO ADULTHOOD

"Accessibility is often misunderstood because it's about a lot more than wheelchair access. Often, when I enter a building, that's all I see."

—From my article on accommodating disabilities in the workplace (Richings, 2020b)

Chapter 6

Adapting to New Healthcare and Support Challenges

Aging out of my dad's health insurance

As I already mentioned, I grew up in the Canadian health system, in the province of Ontario. For people with disabilities, it's not the worst place to be. It has a lot in common with the NHS, because it's a publicly funded system, where taxpayer dollars cover most of the costs. If you file paperwork that proves you cannot work because of your disability, or you live in poverty, some social programs will cover the cost of medication.

If you're working, insurance is sometimes available through your job. Insurance covers the costs related to privatized services such as pharmaceuticals, massage, physio and occupational therapy, and dentistry. Although insurance is not a guarantee.

I'm forever grateful for being diagnosed when I was a child, because the occupational therapy and physiotherapy I needed was covered through the family health insurance plan of ACTRA[1] (Ontario Society of Occupational Therapists). Legally, you can be on your family's health insurance plan until your 26th birthday. When I turned 26, I was told that I could no longer access my

---

1   The Canadian performing arts union for professional actors that work in theatre, film, and television.

dad's health insurance. I then had no insurance of my own, but had a Professional Writer's Association of Canada membership. They had their own insurance program, but I couldn't afford it. That same year, a bad night of back pain became a chronic issue. Then I waited way too long to access everything from massage to physiotherapy.

Occasionally, my family offered to pay for these services I was avoiding. I hate nothing more than being a burden to my family, so I said no to their offers far more than I said the word yes.

Eventually, I went to the weekend drop-in clinic at my local community health center.[2] Chronic back pain was wreaking havoc on my sleep schedule, and I couldn't cope with the pain on my own. When I finally spoke to a nurse practitioner, she asked me if I had health insurance. When I said no, she referred me to an onsite physiotherapist. Since it was at the local community health center, I could at least access government subsidized care (Government of Ontario, 2017).

On a weekly basis, my physiotherapist coached me through exercises and pain management tactics. My physiotherapist was a spry Latino woman who wore a metallic cross around her neck. She looked old enough to be my aunt or mother. So, her instructions came across as maternal, firm, and compassionate. She also had the physical appearance of an Olympic athlete specializing in track and field.

When I told her about my dyspraxia, she did her best to make her instructions dyspraxia-friendly. When I couldn't understand the instructions, she grabbed the leg or arm that needed to move in a specific direction. Then she gently led me in the right direction. She had so much physical strength that this was something she could do effortlessly. When that didn't work, she would show me pictures and videos of what I was supposed to be doing. She taught me a ton of helpful yoga stretches and coping

---

2   Community health centers are Canadian healthcare institutions where the staff gets government paycheques on a per patient/per appointment basis for members of a specific neighbourhood or community.

mechanisms for combating the pain. For the very first time, I felt like I could fight the pain without reaching for the nearest bottle of pain killers.

After a while, I couldn't keep up. The pace and demand of the therapy process was getting too overwhelming. Attending my appointments on a regular basis got way too difficult, even though this wasn't my first experience with physiotherapy.

When I was a kid, I took occupational and physiotherapy for granted. A few years before we got married, my husband had back surgery for the scoliosis he had lived with since he was a kid. Due to post-surgical complications, he had additional surgeries for sepsis, and unusually slow skin healing. Since his surgeries affected his mobility, he also had to get physiotherapy and occupational therapy. As I was a regular visitor, I would often watch the physio and occupational therapists do their work. The first time I had needed their help, I was only four years old, so I never really grasped the motivations behind the activities and exercises they were asking me to do. This was the very first time I truly understood the motivations and purpose of their work.

Occupational therapists and physiotherapists help people who have experienced everything from neurological disabilities to injuries that make motor skills and movement-based tasks challenging. Although I have met plenty of dyspraxics who have never had physiotherapy or occupational therapy, I'm a huge believer in its benefits. As part of my dyspraxia, I have always lived with hypotonia: impairment of the instinct to release muscle tension when you're trying to relax. Hypotonia combined with DCD's spatial awareness and coordination elements create one very large package of stumbly awkwardness; physiotherapy helps you take a lot more effective control of your body, mind, and environment.

Occupational therapy taught me how to operate inanimate objects without hurting myself or other people. This is exactly why physiotherapy and occupational therapy need to be accessible to all. The lack of access to support is a class-based issue, and so few books, studies, and conferences on this subject acknowledge this problem.

The ones who can access it either have access to decent social programs or they can afford to pay for it. If you can't access support, you must live without a formal diagnosis, or proper support. A lack of support has a damaging effect on mental health, which is a common, coexisting condition for neurodiverse people.

Studies have shown that neurodiverse people are a lot more likely to develop mental health issues such as anxiety and depression (Kirby, 2021). The mental health aspect[3] is something I'm always paying close attention to because I have a very anxiety-prone brain.

Identifying the support you need

Aging out of the system is about a lot more than just insurance. It's also about what happens when you go from being a child, protected and advocated for in the local school system, to an adult expected to make decisions about your best interests.

I was one of the lucky ones who had no issues whatsoever with getting a diagnosis or the therapy I needed. The hardest part was becoming an adult, and no longer having the level of support that I once did. Writer Beth Arky (2019) explored this topic in the context of autism and adulthood, but I genuinely feel that the challenges she's articulating apply to dyspraxics as well: "This forced transition, called 'aging out,' pushes them into the woefully lacking system for disabled adults. And it's not just those with more severely disabled children who are worried."

Taking part-time continuing education classes at George Brown College was my first time experiencing this first-hand. The program I was enrolled in was designed for working adults interested in print and web-based editing. When I reached out to

---

3   I talk about this in more detail in Chapter 12, which focuses exclusively on mental health.

the department that handles the needs of adults with disabilities, they asked how they could help. With a lack of support from experts in the field, I realized that I no longer knew how they could help. What I needed in my adulthood was completely different than what I needed from childhood to my early twenties.

Since I didn't know that at the time, I chose an accommodation that I had from kindergarten to my final year of university: more time, and an alternative testing environment. I let go of that accommodation once I realized that it was no longer helpful for me. I was juggling way too much at once and doing everything at the last minute. Keeping track of important deadlines proved to be more difficult than I remembered and I wasn't absorbing information as effectively as I wanted to. I had to do one of my courses twice to pass the course, and then go through severe burnout to pass the rest of my courses and still run a freelance content writing business.[4]

The last-straw incident was when I had my placement required to pass the program rejected. I took the initiative to find the perfect placement. The administrator said no, because no one had told me that the administrator was supposed to choose my placement. They also had full control over the timing of that placement. I had never felt so unsupported, and I was struggling to thrive because of it. In the end, I dropped out of the program for the sake of my mental health.

When I think big picture about being self-employed and having dyspraxia, I still feel like there's a lack of support available in all aspects of my life. On a psychological level, this has created a lack of trust for government and bureaucracy. To this day, when I talk to bureaucrats about everything from ID renewal to taxes, I always assume that my best interests won't be taken seriously.

Since I'm physically active and independent, I no longer have a fear of stigma. That fear of stigma has been replaced with a

---

4   I discuss my experiences with self-employment (and other types of employment) in the next chapter.

constant need to prove that I deserve disability accommodations and support. I want to be optimistic and see this as a sign of progress, although being optimistic is challenging when the processing part of my dyspraxia is at its worst. Far too many people underestimate just how much that help is needed, despite their good intentions. They don't think that what I'm facing is serious, and don't really know what they can do to help.

For the most part, this challenge is both a blessing and a curse. My coping methods have gotten so good that people are surprised when I say I have a disability. I also have years of practice with doing things that make me seem like a person who doesn't have a neurological disability. Caring about my appearance and staying in shape has given me an above-average level of self-awareness. I always know when my disability is on the verge of creating some sort of issue, and what to do about it. In all environments, this creates a protective shield that helps me "blend in."

The hardest part, though, is when this completely fails. Then, I face the challenges and consequences of neurological differences. Water instead of milk ends up in the cereal bowl, and my foot gets so tangled up in objects that I fall over or break something. Sometimes, I can't remember what people said to me a few minutes ago. I always feel at my most self-conscious when I realize that this is the twentieth time that someone has repeated crucial instructions. Very few people react with anything else besides impatience, and that's when I feel extremely disabled.

Chapter 7

How Having a Disability Motivated My Decision to Pursue Self-Employment

The dyspraxic brain is like an internet browser with multiple tabs open. Each "tab" represents some sort of noise or distraction. As the tabs increase, you get less and less capable of keeping track of where you're going and what you're doing. When I'm unable to control my environment, the "tabs" exceed what I can realistically handle. Then my brain goes into a state of extreme focus and concentration, which drains my energy and makes it hard to concentrate on instructions and casual conversations.

For me, this has been the biggest challenge of finding and maintaining long-term employment. People I work with must be willing to accommodate the challenges of my disability. Uptimize, an organization that provides neurodiversity training, demonstrated exactly what is needed to make a workplace neuroinclusive.[1] According to Lauren Hawthorne, the marketing director of Uptimize:

There is generally little fear of not being able to do a good job and contribute – but there is a concern about not being

---

1   Neuroinclusive environments are places where neurodiverse people are not only included, but work in an environment where they can truly thrive.

understood and accepted. Many feel the need to 'mask' their differences, leading to significant effort and exhaustion while doing so. (Hawthorne, 2021)

In countries such as Canada, the U.K., and the U.S.A., some policies are in place to prevent workplace discrimination. In Britain, there is the Access to Work program, which provides practical and financial support for people with disabilities (Department for Work and Pensions, 2021). In America, there's the Americans with Disabilities Act (ADA: see ADA National Network, 2019), which protects disabled people from discrimination and ensures that they can access the same opportunities as everyone else. In Canada, legal protections such as the Charter of Rights and Freedoms provide rights and protections that are a lot like the ADA's protections for disabled people (Canadian Civil Liberties Association, 2018).

However, this doesn't completely get rid of stigma in the pre- and post-hiring process. Maxwell Dean, a marketing and content executive at The Autism Directory managed to find the root of the problem: "Ultimately, before anyone can communicate confidently in the workplace, they must feel they are being listened to" (Dean, 2020).

When I was a teenager working for the very first time, the fear of stigma was widely prevalent. Neurodiversity training was not yet a popular thing, and the only accessible resources contained terminology with negative assumptions attached to it such as "disorder." I was so junior that asking for accommodations and support made me feel like a burden and an inconvenience. I had not yet earned anyone's respect. So my head was filled with toxic ideas about not "deserving" support. My superiors were a major part of why so many toxic ideas about "not deserving" help floated through my head. I genuinely believed that there was always too much work to do and too little time to request accommodations or support.

My first ever work experience happened at the Royal Ontario

Museum's children's program where I was part of a team of people taking care of other people's children for the day. The average age of the kids was six, and they called everyone over the age of 12 "mommy" or "daddy". Working at a children's program is a year-round camp counsellor role. One minute, you're trying to figure out who "started it" in a dispute between two kids; the next minute you're teaching a large group of kids a new game or activity. Since I'm a person with a sensory and coordination disorder, this wasn't an ideal environment.

It was a fun experience, but I had to dedicate the same level of energy to staff "check-in" meetings at the end of the day. At these meetings, I had no energy left to give, and I was getting along with the kids better than the staff. When my boss suddenly and persistently started to tell me that I needed to "smile more," it stung a little bit. I was doing my job properly and wasn't doing anything wrong. During the workday, looking out for my own spatial awareness while keeping a crowd of children safe, and dealing with museum guests and parents drained my energy. In fact, I was doing what I could to thrive in that environment.

Often, my dyspraxic brain is at its worst when I experience stress or exhaustion. In stressful situations, I lose control and my coping mechanisms are inaccessible. Then, everything gets a lot harder to keep track of.

Despite everything I just mentioned, I stayed at the Royal Ontario Museum for multiple seasons. I am good with kids, and taking care of them gave me a sense of purpose. A lot of people have told me that my love of storytelling and my tendency to treat everyone as an equal help me get along with children of all age groups.

Back then, I was also babysitting a lot of kids of local actors, filmmakers, journalists, and musicians. That's the main reason why the Canadian National Exhibition was a regular summer job for me for such a long time. My ability to connect with kids made me a children's program asset. However, at the Canadian National Exhibition I connected with the kids far better than I connected with the adults. I had a limited amount of energy to expend at end of the day and put minimal effort into my relationships with my colleagues. Outside of work, I was heavily immersed in solitary activities, such as reading and short story writing. So, I was a lot more interested in the things I was creating.

I used to think that working with kids was the only thing I was good at. Then I started to do everything from office and research work to audio transcription and social media marketing. With office work, I could at least put headphones on and work for hours on end. I put so much energy and focus into the work that I spent very little time making friends with colleagues, which triggered an unnecessary amount of stigma and anxiety.

As I got older, one very important thing did not change: I never managed to find anything that had full-time hours. I took jobs where I was living an independent contractor-like lifestyle before I was an independent contractor. I would jump from one temporary opportunity to the next.

After college, I applied for jobs with full-time hours, and it didn't go all that well. Sometimes, I would get interviews, and sometimes I would undersell myself in the application. I openly admit that I take things a bit too literally sometimes, and that often works against me. Answering questions under pressure in environments such as job interviews has never been a strength of mine. So, I'd provide answers to interview questions that didn't represent what I was capable of.

Eventually, I gave up on getting a non-remote job. So, self-employment was a logical and natural step. I was only 22 years old when I first started to work for myself. I had no peers, community, or resources to guide me on my journey. All I really had was confidence in my strengths, determination, and people who were willing to pay for my knowledge of blogs, social media, and websites. Most of the time I felt like a huge imposter; I was googling my way through every problem, but I got the work done anyways. Ever since, I've never left the self-employed, work-from-home lifestyle.

The main attraction of this lifestyle was the massive amount of control I had over my work environment. Before that, I was unable to access low-stimuli environments where I could choose if I work in solitude or talk to people. This was a big part of what made me start writing at such a young age. A year before my university graduation, I wrote in my diary reflecting on an important realization that I had. This realization heavily influenced my interest in self-employment:

> I almost wonder if this writing gift of mine is because I'm not meant to experience certain things but just listen, watch, and record stories and other means of communication, and objectively analyze in a way no one else can.

However, that opinion took some time to come to fruition. When I was a kid, I watched my parents struggle through the early years of being creative professionals who are just starting out. I loved to write and realized it was my greatest strength.

Through my parents, I learned that I had to do a lot much more than just write. So, I learned other skills and gained experience doing other things. Writing seemed like a tough thing to gravitate toward right away, and I never felt at ease in work environments that diversified my experiences. I got excluded from social events and missed out on opportunities. I also thought the only way to survive was not to talk about my disability. So, no one knew what I was going through. This left me in a constant bind of not wanting to be treated differently, while having a brain that isn't wired in a neurotypical way. Sometimes I needed things to be explained in a different way, and I didn't know how to ask for help on my own.

Not disclosing my diagnosis led to an unnecessary number of questions about awkward behavior and an inability to process instructions at a "normal" rate. I lived in too much shame for far too long to tell everyone about my disability. The issue, really, was the social circle I grew up in. To this day, conversations about accessibility make me cringe. Accessibility is often discussed with a very black-and-white approach to disabilities in mind. It's a worldview that looks at disabilities purely based on mobility: you either can't walk without a mobility device, such as a wheelchair or cane, or you don't have a disability and "should" stop complaining.

Disclosing your disability to others places you in an unwanted box of expectations. There are certain things people think you can do and certain things they think you can't do. So, they talk slower and expect less out of you.

As soon as I had a university degree in my hand, other people's expectations rose. This made it easier for people to take both me and my disability seriously. Being taken seriously has always been a struggle, and for such a long time this didn't feel like an achievable goal. Once I achieved that goal, I had a whole new set of expectations and challenges. Sometimes, though, other people's expectations are higher than what I can realistically achieve.

The more I gain experiences, the more I feel a sense of shame and disappointment when people believe in me. These days, when I tell others about my disability, the go-to question is always "What can I do to help?" However, I don't always want help. In fact, even if it seems like I'm struggling, sometimes the right level of help is patience and understanding.

Chapter 8

Developing Healthy Relationships

Dyspraxia, at its worst, isn't sexy. Most of the time you're as awkward and clumsy as a drunk after closing time. At its best, you're still experiencing the same frustrations, but you have some control over your movements. Unfortunately, this meant that my earliest experiences with sexuality were equally awkward.

My first crush was someone I went to arts camp with. Only a year before that, I hit puberty. So, I still don't know if it was a crush in the conventional sense of the word. It might have also been a straightforward desire to connect on an emotional level with a like-minded human being. At arts camp, we were casual friends putting on plays and participating in arts and crafts activities. It was when we ended up at the same school that things got difficult.

Everyone knew I was different, odd, and a bit awkward, but I did not have the courage or words to say what was wrong with me. Then my actions got misinterpreted, and an ugly rumor that I was stalking my crush ostracized me from most of my peers. No matter how hard I tried to prove them wrong, no one, including my immediate group of friends, would take my point of view seriously.

A year later, high school started, and this rumor was unresolved. A friend of mine tricked me into thinking that she was going to help me, but instead she became the girlfriend of the guy I was desperately trying to resolve this rumor with. I thought she was helping me, but she was just trying to be this guy's girlfriend.

I was so mad at her that I told her that we couldn't be friends anymore. Unsuccessfully, she tried to turn the whole school against me.

The only reason she was unsuccessful was because my brother transferred from the high school he originally enrolled in to my high school that year. So, I was once again subject to his loving, yet firm, protection. I also had a small group of guys my age who were always looking out for my best interests. Eventually, the girl I ended a friendship with broke up with her boyfriend, and had no friends left.

Back then, the only women I interacted with were book-smart people who didn't quite fit in. So, I believed that dating was for popular guys and girls, who looked like supermodels, wore trendy clothes, and had perfect skin. Since that wasn't me, and I knew that this would never be me, I put my high IQ and book-smarts before my sexuality.

After all that time, I thought I was the only one who faced the challenges I faced, and this had a negative impact on my peer relationships. No one really understood why I couldn't express my thoughts and feelings in large group settings. Getting into university was my priority, and I had no interest in parties or the school dance.

When I was a teenager, everyone knew what depression was. It was an enlightened era; seeing a therapist or knowing someone who attempted suicide was unavoidable. In fact, one of my first secondary school friends would self-harm on a regular basis, and she had anorexia. Most of my peers understood what that meant, although I was the only person who accepted my friend despite those challenges. We immediately bonded over our shared experiences of feeling like social outcasts amongst our peers.

Everyone I knew had some understanding of ADHD. In fact, one of the most popular guys in school had ADHD. Dyspraxia, on the other hand, was never a discussion topic. Even the most experienced educators didn't really understand it.

When I tried to explain my disability to others, everyone

would think that I had ADHD. In fact, my disability would often get miscategorized as something that affected my social and emotional development. Every report card had comments about how I didn't "participate enough," but what they were really picking up on was my introversion. Reading books and quietly reflecting has always been my natural impulse. For such a long time, my teachers rewarded people with the loudest voice rather than the loudest mind.

How going to university helped me learn to be proud of my disability

On July 26th, 1990, the Americans with Disabilities Act came into effect. Every July, ever since, the disability community has celebrated disability pride on an international level. It took so many years for me to feel the same sense of pride about my own disability as the event's average participant. Overcoming that sense of shame was something I had to do to truly feel like meaningful healthy relationships of all kinds were an achievable goal.

My university years were a safe period of my life, where I could slowly figure out how best to speak up about my disability and not feel like I had to apologize about it. Everyone around me was either "coming out" as gay or having an open conversation about their mental health struggles. In my first year of college, a high percentage of my friends were diagnosed with depression or had their first nervous breakdown. They were loved, supported, and encouraged to seek the help they deserved. More importantly, though, this didn't make them less popular. This supportive environment is what changed my perception of disabilities in general.

When I was in university, I was also sending poetry manuscripts and job applications to more places than I can count. Rejection was an ongoing part of my life. After a while, I experienced so much rejection that I wasn't afraid of hearing the word "no." If I wanted to go after a person, opportunity, or thing I simply went for it and adjusted my action plan based on people's reactions.

What held me back from being truly happy in all kinds of relationships?

Soon after college, I was in a monogamous relationship with a man who eventually became my husband. By our first date, we were both talking on a deep emotional level about our disabilities openly. For hours, we also talked about key subjects like our families and our extremely similar tastes in music and movies. That's when I knew I had something special.

From puberty up until I met my husband, I've had my heart broken by boys I didn't deserve or need. I still had so much to learn about what I wanted and needed, and I needed more time to get to know myself first. Living with a disability that has a low level of awareness can do terrible things to your self-esteem.

When I look back, I realize it's based on something quite primal: the outrageous notion that from a reproduction point of view, not being perfectly able-bodied and -minded makes you a less attractive prospect to a potential mate. Then, something inside you festers—a mindset that makes you believe that only "certain people" are worthy of love. Next thing you know, you're surrounded by toxic people who only want you to solve their problems. This leads to less time and energy for people who care about your best interests.

The biggest barrier to meaningful relationships: Other people's expectations

Chronic illnesses are a death sentence in some countries.[1] In some cases, the death sentence aspect applies to low-income

---

1   The fatal aspects globally are coexisting factors like lack of access to proper treatment and care, and coexisting mental health issues, I have found that this is just as much of a factor in the U.S.A., Canada, and the U.K., as it is in middle- and low-income countries due to the greed of corporations and government officials. Sadly, this is making a lot of disabled people feel like a burden not only to their families but to potential long-term romantic partners due to awareness of the costs and time required to support them.

countries: chronic illnesses make it harder and more expensive to marry off young women. However, I've met an increasing number of people from the U.S. as well who have lost their children, spouses, and siblings due to a lack of access to affordable medication, treatment, and care.

The widespread popularity of ableism in our society has led to a lot of disabled people absorbing this toxic mentality, leading to self-esteem, confidence, and body-image issues, and shielding them from happiness. Often doctors, educators, friends, and family will claim that we'll have a shorter lifespan and miss out on life's most important milestones. Since these are often people we trust, far too many disabled people must unlearn this belief; we're de-sexualized and stigmatized by people who don't really get us but claim to be looking out for our best interests.

Far too many dyspraxia stories highlight trauma from romantic partners, friends, and family who refuse to take dyspraxia seriously. When dyspraxia isn't taken seriously by the people we trust, trauma happens. Relationship-based trauma is a major barrier that stops dyspraxics from trusting people and seeking support. More people need to listen, and far fewer people need to simply assume they know better.

Some positive relationship advice

These days, I truly believe that people who aren't willing to accept the unflattering parts of my dyspraxia aren't worth my time or energy. This may sound like a common-sense principle to some readers, but it took me so many years to internalize this belief.

In the early days of the COVID-19 pandemic, I talked to a dyspraxic young woman at a Zoom-based event on dyspraxia coping mechanisms. Her face was glowing a bright shade of red, and she mentioned she was in a new relationship. When I asked her if she had told her boyfriend about her dyspraxia she smiled and nodded. Since she was a lot younger than me, I was so happy for her. She was experiencing something I wanted so badly at her age: unconditional love and acceptance. So, I made a huge point of sharing with her what worked in the most successful and meaningful relationship I've ever had.

Ever since we first started dating, my husband and I have been adapting to the strengths and weaknesses of our disabilities. We transparently communicated what we do and don't need, which has helped us both adapt to each other's strengths and weaknesses without operating on assumptions alone. For example, my clumsiness and tendency to get lost on the way to my destination became a normal part of our lives. Important instructions are verbally expressed in low-stimuli environments with whatever visual aids we can find. With my husband's diabetes, I've adapted to things like "apple juice o'clock" and muttered words being a sign of low blood sugar. Everywhere we go, I'm always helping him carry things and making sure that his needs are respected. Ever since his back surgery, he walks with a cane, and he needs my help with carrying heavy bags of groceries and laundry.

You need to get comfortable with the idea that you will find some household tasks difficult, and in serious, long-term relationships you will sometimes have to ask your partner for help. A great example is the task of cooking and the shame that dyspraxic women often experience for finding it difficult. A large amount of spatial processing, awareness, and coordination is involved in preparing a meal. So that's quite common. When I was a guest panelist on a Dyspraxic Women's Network YouTube Live all the panelists, along with many of the people who contributed to the live chat, had a story about this. However, if both parties (in the relationship) clearly communicate with their partner what they need without having their needs ignored, the relationship will be a healthy one. Anyone who doesn't listen to or respect your needs isn't worth it.

PART III

LIVING WITH DYSPRAXIA

"To give neurodiversity the recognition it deserves, neurodiverse people need to control the narrative of how others talk about their disability. We need so much more than just one tweet, quoted without consent for this to happen."

—A passage from my Medium Digest-based open letter response to an article published in *The Independent* (Richings, 2021)

Chapter 9

The Effect of Stigma on Self-Esteem and Body Image

I'm from an unusually fit and physically active family. My brother is in the military, my father is a professional actor who sees staying fit as part of his job, and my mother values the idea of staying fit.

Staying fit has helped me keep up with my family's hyperactive energy. It has also helped me cope with the harder parts of dyspraxia, such as social anxiety, and the intense emotions that I feel when experiencing sensory overload. I had to find a fitness activity that works for me and allows me to progress at my own pace, something that dyspraxia makes unnecessarily complicated. I've experienced a lifetime of stigma in group fitness settings, and that severely limits what fitness activities I can participate in. A great example of this is a diary entry I wrote when I was 12 years old, which demonstrates just how much of a nightmare PE class was for me when I was in school:

> *Today was so frustrating in my gym class for me and my team-mates. It all started when our gym teacher introduced a game. "Okay class, this game will have 4 teams. Each team will number*

off the players from 1 to 5," he said. The second I walked over to my teammates was when our loss began. After a while, he called number 5 (me). He explained what we had to do, and that's when it got even worse. Even though it was a chest pass for basketball "easy," the bad luck spread like bread and butter on someone else's turn. We had to pass the ball to every member of the team. Unfortunately, I was having so much trouble figuring out how to do chest passes that our team lost.[1]

Due to my lack of hand-eye coordination, any team sport that requires catching or throwing a ball is inaccessible. After very little time, my peers caught on to how bad I was at sports. I was picked last for every team sport. Our teacher wanted everyone to participate, but no one wanted me on their team. I didn't want to be on their team either. Instead, I looked forward to the times when the teacher asked us to do laps. I was the only person in my class who was good at running, and that's all I really wanted to do during gym class.

I had an above average level of endurance, and a group of guys in my gym class eventually realized that I was good at defense in both field hockey and football. In fact, I was better at defense than most of the women in my class.

When I was only 13 years old, I made an appointment with the school administration. I wanted to replace my gym class time with a special education class and needed the approval of the school administrator. I found a way to be fit and physically active on my own. Having to keep with my peers' own version of their personal best was causing me nothing but stress. Some of the students who had access to special education were taking special education classes instead of third language classes. So, having my request approved didn't seem impossible.

---

1   Diary entry from November 5th, 2003.

I went to King Edward Public School, which is walking distance from Toronto's Little Italy and Chinatown neighborhoods. To accommodate King Edward's multicultural identity, students could take not only French, but one other language as well. Options included Spanish, Mandarin, and Cantonese. I loved the idea of taking beginner Spanish. I had a youth YMCA membership at the time, and many of the personal trainers that worked at the YMCA were native Spanish speakers, who patiently taught me how to use the machines and weight room. Instructions were conveyed through demonstrations and not being afraid to guide my hand, arm, or leg in the right direction if I was doing something wrong. Repeatedly, the staff taught me the same set of instructions until they were satisfied with how well I was doing.

The staff were so kind to me that being able to say basic phrases like "Hello" and "Good morning" to them in their native language seemed like a kind gesture. In the end, I got exactly what I wanted, formal permission to opt out of PE. Since the gym teacher was also my cross-country and track and field coach, he didn't see this as anything personal. In fact, he encouraged me to train on my own.

By secondary school, I had opted out of gym class by making the same argument. I still had the same fitness routine, and I was on the cross-country and track and field teams. Not having a gym class to go to didn't stop me from staying in shape. Although I missed out on the sexual education focus of health class, I was a book-smart kid who spent a lot of time in the local library. I learned what I needed to know through reading about it and talking to my brother, family, and friends.

In university, high gym membership costs scared me away from gyms, but I was still running. Running helped me feel more in control of my own body and mind, something that I don't experience enough in my personal life:

When I'm tired, dyspraxia sets in really hardcore. I get clumsy and can't process anything. When that happens, I get anxious and upset, because I'm reminded of the lack of control I had pre-occupational therapy. When I run, I feel super powerful because from the start to the finish line I feel like...just for a second, the disability I've had since birth doesn't even exist. And man...the endorphins! The endorphins are great!

However, I quickly realized that my fitness habits are too cardio-focused (swimming, running, and skating exclusively). This created strength imbalance in my body. My legs were strong, but my core strength was weak. Since I assumed all other fitness activities weren't a good fit for me, my strength imbalance problem was ignored for far too long.

Although the massive strength imbalance in my body didn't affect me until my 26th birthday, when I developed chronic back pain issues, I have had a hypotonia diagnosis, a low muscle tone disorder, for just as much time as my dyspraxia. Your muscle tone refers to your body's resistance to stretching when it's resting. Hypotonia essentially means that your muscles don't properly contract in a resting position (NHS, 2021).

My hypotonia was straightforward to manage, and easy to forget about until years of muscular strain started to manifest itself as pain. An article that I wrote for Saatva Mattress company's blog (Richings, 2019a) explored these challenges in deeper detail:

On a scale of 1–10 (with 1 being minimal pain and 10 being the worst pain imaginable), my back pain was an 8 most of the time. Sleeping while I was in so much pain was difficult, and that impacted my focus and productivity. I'm self-employed and interact with a lot of clients—but because sleep deprivation creates irritability and makes it hard to focus, dealing with people was a lot more challenging than it normally is.

Eventually, my doctor referred me to a physiotherapist who taught me basic yoga to strengthen the part of my body that was experiencing pain. This inspired to go to my local community center's indoor pool on a weekly basis during its Leisure Swim time slots. Sometimes, I would go for a Friday evening swim; sometimes, I would go for a Saturday or Sunday afternoon swim; and sometimes, I would go for a swim during both these time slots. A lot just depended on how bad my chronic pain was that day, and what my schedule was that week.

Swimming is a comfortable activity I can do on my own, because I have been swimming since I was a little girl. I took lessons at one point, and it wasn't easy to learn. It took patient instructors showing me how to move in the pool, rather than telling me how to swim, for me to learn the basics. After I stopped going to lessons, I became a better swimmer through practice alone.

I was much better off once I realized my lack of grace in every movement doesn't even matter. In the water, my hands and legs splash so aggressively that water goes everywhere, but I stopped caring about that a long time ago. In the water I'm fast, strong, care-free, and in control of my strengths and weaknesses. Outside of the water, I'm not always in control, and that's a difficult reality to live with.

My hypotonia suddenly getting a lot worse was something I interpreted as a sign that I couldn't just swim and run forever. I had to try something new, even though trying unfamiliar fitness activities are always intimidating for me. After practicing yoga on my own for a while, I gained the confidence that I needed to try the first group fitness class of my adulthood. Eventually, I wrote a Medium Digest-based article (Richings, 2019b) about how trying something new made a difference:

Having a (mediation studio) pass that only lasted two weeks was the motivation that I needed to dedicate myself to my meditation practice. It was the first time since I finished university, where I could just be still and alone with my thoughts for 30 minutes to hour-long increments. So, I experienced a range of emotions that were more intense than what I'd experienced in a while. For instance, in the breathwork class, I cried because it has been so long since someone permitted me to just let stuff go. Then, in Rise (the movement class), every bone in my body cracked, as I released tension in my body triggered by back pain issues.

I had such a great time at the studio that I purchased a membership when the two week-pass expired, and I attended the studio's classes every week. The one that resonated with me the most was their Rise Class. Rise facilitates a judgment-free zone where you're meant to challenge the physical limits of your body, under the careful guidance of a personal trainer. It also seamlessly combines experimental dance and movement, with the instructor's CrossFit, yoga, and meditation influences. The main objective of the Rise class is releasing tension to strengthen every muscle in the body. Since it was in a room with deliberately dim lighting, and an upbeat soundtrack, my anxiety about not being as good as everyone else instantly evaporated.

When I told the instructor about dyspraxia, she knew exactly what it was, and told me stories about her private physical training clients who have dyspraxia. This made me feel much more at ease and made it easier for her to properly accommodate my disability.

Then, the COVID-19 pandemic happened, and the community centers, along with the meditation studio that I attended on a regular basis, were closed. I couldn't access a pool, and I found virtual yoga and meditation in a small apartment extremely difficult. I couldn't get the same results from my workout routine and that was a difficult adjustment to make.

One of my most important coping mechanisms for dyspraxia has always been consistent routines. When COVID started, my routine was disrupted, and my chronic pain came back worse than ever. Some nights, it would be so bad that I wouldn't get enough sleep. When my chronic pain started to come back in waves, I was reminded of the mindset challenges that are closely intertwined with my dyspraxia experience. In fact, I think a diary entry from 2011 articulates this issue perfectly:

> I can't sleep. All these thoughts are bouncing around and this week's a bummer. I'm tired all the time this week and it makes things well...not great because my brain behaves differently. I'm starting to see more links between dyspraxia and the anxieties that keep resurfacing than ever before. It's all related, that's my conclusion and I'd give anything for it to go away. There's a doubting side of me that's barely getting by, and I want to do better. I'm so behind on certain things in my life, and other things in my life keep getting in the way, and more and more time just keeps passing by. And I'm always so tired, and rejection just keeps slapping me in the face. It's just really frustrating how I keep trying really hard on things these days, and it doesn't amount to anything at all.[2]

Often, the dyspraxia community has talked about how hard you must work to achieve the same things as people who don't have dyspraxia. Most of the people who work in the health and wellness industry sell their classes as the magic pill solutions, but they don't realize how inaccessible their activities can be. Activities like going to the gym are often sold as the right thing for everyone to do. What that's failing to consider is just how

---

2   Diary entry from November 9th, 2011.

inaccessible a fast-paced Zumba class or even a serene yoga class might be to a person with DCD.

That's exactly why my first group yoga class didn't go well. We were supposed to be following the instructions with our eyes closed. Since I process verbal instructions at a slower pace than the average person, I misunderstood the instructions and hurt my back. Also, my mother came with me, who has more yoga experience than I do, and occasionally she would open her eyes and tell me I was doing the exercises wrong. Meanwhile, I was disobeying the instructor's wishes for everyone to close their eyes. This seemed to be the only way for me to at least try to keep up. So, I had no other choice.

I have been always aware of the subtle differences in how I move my arms and legs: my tendency to awkwardly stumble through space and time, and the stiff movements of my arms and legs. But in front of me was a woman who represented some of my biggest insecurities. She was shorter, skinnier, and more flexible than me. At first, I saw her as a model for how I should do yoga, but paying attention to this woman made me feel like I don't belong.

It took years to realize where my insecurities were coming from, but eventually I realized that the trashy teen pop culture magazines I read in my adolescence were a bad influence on me. Through these magazines, I was bombarded with advertisements for everything from women's clothing and jewelry to makeup and hair products. None of the women in the photos looked like me, but the women I went to school with looked a lot more like them. They were paper-thin, walked with their head held high, and dressed like Lululemon models.

In time, I rebelled against the messaging and got into everything from *Emily the Strange*, a gothic cartoon character with her own fashion line, to punk rock. Despite all that, I internalized the same insecurities.

Women who looked, walked, and talked like the women in the magazines I grew up with had easy access to good opportunities with minimal effort. Despite hard work and perseverance, a large chunk of the world seemed inaccessible to me. I didn't look like any of the women who seemed to have it all figured out, and I felt like I was doing something wrong. Then, along came a clothing line for women who look like me. This heightened my confidence and changed my perception of my neurological differences.

By 2018, advertising executives had started to catch on to the growing level of acceptance toward disability and mental health. One of the first brands to jump on the bandwagon was Aerie. Aerie embraced diversity by hiring women to model their clothing of all body types, skin colors, and backgrounds, along with women with visible disabilities. Through its ad campaigns, Aerie communicates a powerful message. Aerie is for *all* women. However, for this to not be exploitative, it must be approached in the right way.

Based on how Aerie's models felt about how the campaign was handled from the inside, its message is 100 percent genuine. Many of the models have struggled with self-acceptance because of the physical and mental effects that come with their conditions. So, they saw Aerie's message of acceptance as a positive platform for eliminating stigma and empowering women with similar medical conditions.

All models involved in this campaign saw their work as a positive platform for empowering other women (Callahan, 2018). For this very reason, the message came across as genuine. The success of the Aerie campaign is based on its most unique achievement. Since 2018, it has attracted a demographic of young women who don't identify with the skinny, able-bodied models who wear the lingerie sold at most major retailers.

After my first yoga class, physical pain and feeling vulnerable made me resort back to familiar insecurities. Next thing I knew I was taking out my frustrations on a woman who wears a smaller-sized pair of yoga pants than I do. One week later, I saw the same woman at my Rise class, and she mentioned it was her first time at this class. Since I was a regular student of this class, I decided to give her some advice on what to expect. This advice clearly made a difference, and she thanked me for helping her feel reassured. Suddenly, she wasn't an embodiment of my insecurities. She was someone who reminded me of the struggles and challenges I've faced when trying new fitness activities.

Exercise is good for you, but the class sizes and pace of group fitness classes are often too fast. I realize asking for smaller class sizes and more one-on-one instruction is probably a lot to ask. Instead, we need to encourage people to gravitate toward activities that they're not only good at, but like. If this approach is encouraged, far fewer people will have a negative view of going outside and getting some exercise.

From an accessibility perspective, a step in the right direction was the Cripple Punk Movement:

> Plug the term into Google and you'll see an explosion of hits: people taking Instagram-style selfies with their walkers and canes in full view, confessional text posts about doctor's appointments, blogs dispensing advice on dealing with new pain medications and photos of canes painted with blue polka dots and tentacles.
>
> This is the essence of cripple punk: an uncensored, unapologetic look into the lives of disabled people who are tired of being your pity porn. (Drmay, 2016)

The Cripple Punk Movement has shown that accessibility has a long way to go before all members of the disability community feel included. In 2018, 'Crip Punk' exploded in popularity on Tumblr and other social media platforms. Most of the participants resembled the 1970s punks of my parents' generation. The only real difference was the social cause that fueled this movement. Participants in this movement were proudly normalizing the disability experience. People with canes and wheelchairs, who looked like vintage punk album covers, became powerful advocates for accessible concert venues. Another key participant in that movement was the chronic illness community, who used platforms like Instagram to de-stigmatize the hospital waiting room experience.

Cripple Punk challenges the doctor- and academic-dominated disability narrative through focusing on disability pride and activism. Members of the movement put themselves front and center, unafraid of people's misconceptions about their disability. This seems like a small thing, but it isn't. If you pay close attention to contemporary politics, you'll realize that the people who have all the power rarely have disabilities. This has led to laws being passed that don't properly accommodate the needs of the disability community.

Why the stigma you're facing isn't just a phase, and what to do about it

Mindset shifts don't completely get rid of stigma. The fear of stigma has always been there for everything I've done, from starting new jobs to making new friends.

The fear of stigma is always there for one very specific reason: there are far too many misconceptions out there about what living with dyspraxia is really like. The presence of people with disabilities in advertisements and TV shows is a sign of progress, but there are still far too many negative assumptions and expectations.

Progressive institutions like universities have also internalized this behavior. When I was applying for university, I experienced this first-hand. At the university and college fair, I asked a lot of questions about how students with disabilities are accommodated. This helped me filter out universities with indifferent attitudes toward students with disabilities. When all I got was someone rolling their eyes at me in response to my questions, I didn't bother to apply. There's a very real reason why I took this approach: you never really know how people will react when talking about a hidden condition like dyspraxia.

When I say to someone for the very first time, "I have a disability," my heart rate rises. Suddenly, my mind starts to race, and I expect the worse. Even the nicest and most good-hearted people have made me expect the worst: being treated differently and feeling excluded from everyday activities.

Then, there are the traits of my disability that may affect people's first impressions, like getting lost easily and having no hand–eye coordination or spatial awareness. However, there are ways to compensate that make it possible to overdeliver on promises.

The British member of parliament Emma Lewell-Buck is an openly dyspraxic politician. As a Canadian with a father who was born in the U.K., I've always had a strong emotional connection to the U.K. While Brexit was still being debated amongst British politicians, a dyspraxia awareness week interview with Emma Lewell-Buck showed up online. Before that, I couldn't name a single politician with dyspraxia. Once I listened to Emma's interview, it all started to make a lot of sense; when she spoke in parliament, I spotted familiar coping mechanisms. To thrive in a high-stimuli environment, Emma writes everything down, so that she doesn't forget what she's trying to say. She also memorizes landmarks so that she doesn't get lost on her way to work (Laitner, 2016).

I found out about Emma at a time when I was questioning a lot of my life choices and wanted to do a lot better. Even with an impressive writing portfolio and blog, nothing that I was doing seemed good enough.

These days, I spend so much time with other disabled people that the fear factor is gone, not to mention being self-employed reducing the level of stigma. Getting the job done is all that matters. I never quite know how potential clients will respond to my disability, and I mention my disability when it's a relevant contribution to the project that I'm working on.

When I compared my experience to Emma Lewell-Buck's story, I immediately noticed that she is a passionate voice not only for the disability community, but also for families living in poverty. This is a major part of what makes her so popular. However, I also remember her expressing concern in one of her interviews about people thinking disability-related issues are all that matters to her. This couldn't be more inaccurate, but it is an assumption she feared her colleagues would make if they knew about her disability.

Just like Emma Lewell-Buck, I have learned to cope with dyspraxia by writing and rehearsing important things I want to say. This has helped me do everything from facilitate Zoom calls, to asking the right questions during consultation calls with new clients. I also plan my life around getting lost, because even the most familiar places can confuse me. All it really takes for me to have no idea where I am is the subtlest scenery changes. The first time I visit a place my brain is always taking mental notes about the tiniest details of street corners. This technique helps me navigate my way around important buildings and street corners.

I have developed practical coping mechanisms, but the fear of stigma is always there. Now, when I tell people about my dyspraxia, it's an important test, rather than a source of shame. If the people I talk to don't like it, they're not worth my time. If they're okay with it, I'm loyal and kind to them in return. That's been the most freeing realization of my adult life so far.

An important moment in (dyspraxia) pop culture

At this point, you might feel a sense of hesitation; you might know a lot less about dyspraxia than you thought you did. So, here's my advice: when in doubt, ask people who live with the condition. Especially if you want to tell a dyspraxic person's story. *Doctor Who* took this approach in 2018 with its 11th season, which introduced Ryan, a protagonist who has dyspraxia.

After it had premiered, the #dyspraxia Twitter community discussed the relatability of the characters in the show. A large percentage of the community were pleased with the results.

I don't even watch *Doctor Who*, but the reaction to Ryan's first appearance made me sit down and watch an episode.

The extreme accuracy of how the writers portrayed the character made me cry tears of joy. This was the very first time a TV show had featured a dyspraxic character. The danger of that, really, was that Ryan would be a one-dimensional representation of dyspraxia, but they made a thoughtful effort to represent DCD in a fair way. According to Elizabeth Cassidy (2018): "The show consulted with the Dyspraxia Foundation, which praised the show's portrayal. *Doctor Who* showrunner, Chris Chibnall, decided to incorporate dyspraxia because his nephew has the condition."

I was a bit skeptical at first about the show casting a non-dyspraxic actor, but his portrayal in episode one was extremely accurate. Just like me, Ryan couldn't learn how to ride a bike without hurting himself.

Despite his dyspraxia, Ryan was a key ally for Doctor Who, and was never an object of pity. His disability wasn't his only personality trait so it never seemed like a lazy plot device, although on Reddit some fans criticized just how little his disability was highlighted as the show progressed. What Reddit users were failing to mention is the true significance of having a dyspraxic character on a popular TV show. Ryan is a role model with dyspraxia that people who don't have the condition can also relate to. His presence on TV normalizes the condition and introduces it to people who would very likely not find out about it in any other context. In fact, after the episode premiered, there was a rise in search engine queries which included the word "dyspraxia."

Ryan's disability is a part of who he is rather than a central plot device. This was an especially crucial message for people who live with the condition but worry about it being a barrier to education, employment, or happiness. Ryan gave the community hope, and that's a small but important win for dyspraxics and their families.

Chapter 10

Coping and Persevering

According to several doctors and nurse practitioners who knew me when I was a teenager, I had anemia symptoms from the moment I got my first period. However, I didn't get a formal diagnosis until I had dramatic visit to an all-day breakfast place with my parents that frightened them.

It was a beautiful, lazy Sunday and we decided to go out for brunch. On one of the hottest days of the year, we waited in a long line-up that was moving at the pace of the average snail. At first, I was doing fine and had a nice chat with my parents. Then, I wasn't.

I started seeing dark spots everywhere I looked. The entire room felt like I was on an amusement park ride. The spinning got faster, and faster, and faster, until I blacked out. When I came to, I was sitting at a table, and one of the waitresses put a glass of orange juice on my table. At first, I was a bit confused. Before I blacked out, I was standing in a line-up.

Gently, the waitress tapped me on the shoulder and asked me if I was alright. I was so unsure of what was happening that just for a moment, I couldn't talk. All I could really manage was a nod. The waitress left, and then my parents approached me, encouraging me to drink the orange juice that was on the table. Then, they told me I had fainted.

Despite the drama, we ordered some food anyways, but there was something very serious we couldn't really ignore; no one knew why I had fainted. Months passed, and sometimes I would still faint at home. My parents took me to a doctor, who recommended blood tests. Several blood tests later, my iron levels were low enough for my doctor to recommend iron supplements. I was just as alarmed as they were, so I took my iron supplements every day. Then, I started to carry Luna bars, a type of granola bar that has high iron content, everywhere I went.

A few years later, I was 18 years old, and it was my first summer of being a college student. The G20 protests were happening in Toronto, and I got close enough to the protests for the cops to ask me to run down a side street; there was a riot going on and it was too dangerous. I saw what the streets looked like after the riots but managed to stay out of trouble. For me, the real trouble happened 24 hours later. I was paler than I ever had been, and dark circles highlighted my eyes. I knew something was wrong when I started to see dark spots and the room spinning far too quickly.

While I was getting breakfast at my parents' house, I fainted on my way down the stairs. My dad caught me just in time and this saved me from damaging my head or falling down the stairs. When I came to, I was in my bed with blankets around my waist. In front of me was a tray of tea, blueberries, and cereal. As I ate, I saw him standing in the hallway making sure that I was alright. After I'd finished breakfast, I put on my most comfortable summer dress, a purple dress with white flowers on it that I still wear. Then, my parents informed me they were going to drive me to the nearest community health clinic and book an appointment.

At the health center, the only person who was available was a nurse practitioner I hadn't met before. They took one look at me, and encouraged me go to St. Joseph's Hospital, the nearest hospital. I was so weak and unwell that I wasn't going to question them or say no.

Coincidentally, St. Joseph's Hospital is also the hospital where I was born, and I ended up one floor above the maternity ward I was born in. This gave me an overwhelming feeling of déjà vu. Everything from the statues of Catholic patron saints to the people walking by looked extremely familiar. I was so out of it that I couldn't form cohesive sentences or maintain a conversation. The room appeared to be spinning, and my parents had to do most of the talking for me. I was the maximum age for the children's ward, but the minimum age for the adult ward. So, I could pick either option. Someone suggested the children's ward, and I passively accepted. I was so unwell that I was willing to take any help I could get.

For two weeks, I was an in-patient who was carefully monitored through blood transfusions and tests. For the first time in my life, relying on the patience and help of others was my only option. I couldn't walk short distances, eat something, or go to the bathroom without feeling too weak to stand up properly. St. Joseph's was also an environment where everyone seemed worse off than I was. I kept apologizing for bothering people every time I needed help with walking to the nearby toilet. I couldn't walk without assistance. I had fought for such a long time to be independent, and I was too proud to give up my independence. In this situation, though, I had no choice but to rely on other people, and that made me panic a bit. All that time in a hospital bed made me think a lot about my dyspraxia, and what made me so uncomfortable with seeking the accommodations and support that I need.

I had only just started to feel independent and in control of my own body and mind, so I badly wanted to ignore dyspraxia's existence. When I was lying in my hospital bed, I saw so many people around me relying on other people's support. Every ounce of shame I had about asking for help started to fade away.

When I look back on what life was like when I was a teenager with dyspraxia, I understand why this is an issue. Convincing Mom and Dad that you don't need them is a constant temptation. Meanwhile, you're barely able to navigate your way through space and time without falling over or breaking something. Sports and some types of clothing are inaccessible, and you stumble your way through every step you take.

For me, this led to a lot of awkward social situations. Sometimes, I got bullied by my peers. Until I finished secondary school, I had to look outside of school to find communities that specialized in the two things that I love the most: theater and writing. These communities were important because they stopped me from giving up on school. They also helped me get good enough grades to go to university. I met like-minded people my age, and no longer felt out of place. Then, I studied at the university level what I was passionate about and got the tools that I needed to monetize my love of writing.

However, this didn't get rid of my anxiety entirely. It took a long-term relationship with my partner, who has multiple disabilities of his own, to get over my anxiety about discussing my disability and its symptoms. Talking about and experiencing the ups and downs of disabilities is so normal to him that it finally started to feel normal to me as well. You don't have to find a partner who understands your disability. Forming some sort of peer group that understands your disability and all other aspects of your personality makes a huge difference, and can make the bad days feel so much better.

Humor: An underrated coping method

I grew up with three sets of wise and resilient grandparents,[1] who were a major influence on my coping mechanisms. None of my grandparents came from money, and most of them never finished secondary school. Instead, they worked extremely hard their entire lives, up until retirement. When my elders faced hard times, they were powerful advocates for the needs of themselves and their families. They also found humor in the biggest challenges. That gift was a huge influence on how I have reacted to my dyspraxia over the years.

One of the ways dyspraxia often manifests itself is through

---

1   Three sets due to grandparental divorce and remarriages.

clumsiness, and an inability to process instructions at a quick enough rate. Both of those aspects are way too easy to laugh at. If I have too much to focus on at once it will end in disaster. Food and drink have been spilled, and plates have been broken. The wiring in my brain makes this a consistent part of my life.

When this happens in social situations, no one else seems to laugh, but people don't feel like they have permission to make light of what's going on. Once I laugh, they laugh, because I'm okay with them laughing at my behavior. Often this happens through self-deprecating comments like: "Silly me, that happens sometimes. I have a spatial processing disability, and it makes me do stuff like this! Isn't that hilarious?"

However, with people who know me extremely well, I laugh at what's going on, and apologize. When dyspraxia is combined with chronic pain, and I have one of my dyspraxia bad days, everything I touch falls to bits. That can get a bit overwhelming, because my control of my own actions starts to fade away. Situations like that aren't funny. They can be quite painful.

Next time you or your dyspraxic friends and family experience similar frustrations, remember the wise words of my late grandmother, Molly Pearl Joy Richings: "Sometimes, you just need to have a good swear." Swearing, at least, is something you can always control, and it feels good.

Chapter 11

Why Do People Rarely Know What Dyspraxia Is?

My campus at York University, Glendon Campus, was the university's main campus before the current main campus (Keele Campus) existed. Thanks to a wealthy couple who died a long time ago, several mansion properties in Toronto's Bayview and Lawrence area were transformed into a functional university campus.

One of the most iconic parts of the campus is Glendon Manor, where movies have been filmed[1] and former students have taken wedding pictures and organized actual weddings. Glendon Manor is next door to a forest and a beautiful rose garden. The exterior is unaffected by the passage of time and looks very Victorian estate-like.

The first time I ventured inside Glendon Manor was when I had my first Accessibility Services appointment. I expected beautiful art on the walls, and a Victorian, *Jane Eyre* vibe. Instead, I found myself inside a place that was very cramped and had a hospital level of sterility, although it was a friendly place that encouraged its staff to take their pets to work. Even though my sense of smell was a lot worse back

---

1   For example, *The Time Traveller's Wife.*

then,[2] I vividly remember the Accessibility Office's powerful yet comforting wet dog smell.

After waiting my turn, an employee I had never met before called my name. She looked like a Hollywood movie take on a school librarian. I also remember her being very round and uncomfortable in her own body in a classically "pregnant woman in the late stage of her pregnancy" sort of way.

As soon as we arrived in her office, she sat down facing me in her leather office chair and asked, "What can I do for you?"

"I have dyspraxia, and I've waited far too long to get proper accommodations," I replied. "Dyspraxia is..."

Instead of letting me finish my sentence, she interrupted me and said, "I used to be an occupational therapist. A lot of my clients had dyspraxia. No need to explain. I can just imagine how challenging this must be for you..."

After a moment of comfortable silence, she asked me a series of questions that helped her determine what I needed to do to get proper accommodations. Documents like psychological assessments, doctors' notes, and the contact information for her colleagues who worked at the Keele Campus were mentioned.

Because of that meeting, I had instructions on how to get this process started. After that meeting, I went from not really knowing how to advocate for myself to knowing exactly what I needed to do to get proper accommodations. I felt comfortable and at ease, but didn't really know what to do about the expense of and huge time investment in getting a more up-to-date psychological assessment.

Luckily, I found a clever loophole. Back then, I had a kind-hearted and understanding doctor, who wrote me a note explaining how my dyspraxia affected me. That turned out to

---

2   Along with dyspraxia and a history of anemia, one of the health conditions I also have is a deviated septum, which gives me a poor sense of smell, due to the passage of air through my nose. Doctors tell me it has something to do with the way my nose naturally sits on my face. The reason my sense of smell has improved over time is unconfirmed at this point.

be good enough documentation, but no one told me how to ask for accommodations once I had the paperwork.

The most common misunderstanding about dyspraxia

During the COVID-19 pandemic, I joined a Zoom-based dyspraxia support group. Everyone had a story about other people's lack of patience, including a woman who shared how her boss responded to her DCD:

> What frustrates me the most is that he thinks I don't listen... I do listen, and I try so hard to process all the information, but it's not always easy to process it all. He thinks I'm slow. He thinks I'm stupid. And I wish there was some way to make him understand that this is not the case.

It took me years to realize this, but this is something that has happen to me multiple times. In noisy and crowded environments, I've experienced this the most. In fact, the amount of information I can realistically absorb in conversations is limited. Then, my brain loses its ability to filter out background noise.

When I worked at the Canadian National Exhibition, a Canadian annual summer theme park event, busy days would mean large crowds and loud noises. Then, everyone would have to reluctantly repeat instructions multiple times.

When I go to the grocery store alone, I'm always either wearing my headphones, or I have my Vibes hi-fidelity earplugs in my ears. The earplugs allow me to hear conversations with the sound of all other forms of background noise turned down. Grocery store environments are too high-stimulus for me. When I don't have my headphones or earplugs on, I get easily overwhelmed and forget where I'm going.

Unfortunately, we live in a world that doesn't view all disabilities as equal. In fact, people with disabilities that you can spot in a crowd are given a permission slip; they can take their time and approach things in a way that feels best to them. When I was first diagnosed, caring adults taught me the coping methods that are still a daily contribution to my life.

On an average day, the public doesn't think of me as someone who "looks disabled," but there are some days when I feel disabled. What really helped me be more accepting and less ashamed of my dyspraxia were the Dyspraxic Panda memes. For the first time, I was laughing rather than feeling sorry for myself about my DCD.

The Dyspraxic Panda memes were originally created by Eli in his early twenties when he was living in France (Dyspraxic Panda, 2015). Eli is dyspraxic. He created the Dyspraxic Panda meme because he wanted a safe forum to talk about his DCD experiences, to help dyspraxics and the people who care about them, and have a good laugh. When people ask me about the most common misconception about dyspraxia, I always think about one of the most memorable Dyspraxic Panda memes: *Oh, you're not disabled, you're just clumsy and a little odd!*

What dyspraxia clumsiness is vs. what other people think it is

Surface clumsiness and having a brain that cannot function if there are too many distractions are two completely different things. When there are too many distractions, dyspraxics cannot process information that non-dyspraxics can process automatically, such as getting from one side of a room to another without falling over. Dyspraxics are different than someone who is accident-prone by nature, due to the wiring in the brain.

The part of the brain that processes the complexities of the physical spaces we find ourselves in every day is underdeveloped in dyspraxics. Therefore, frequent clumsiness is a result of neurological limitations. Griffin Occupational Therapy's explanation of dyspraxia shows that dyspraxic clumsiness is more than meets the eye:

[Dyspraxics] are not just clumsy with their movements. They must also have difficulty either thinking of an idea of what to do and/or figuring out how to do it. Typically, dyspraxia is most obvious with new tasks and in new situations as these require much more planning than familiar tasks. (Griffin Occupational Therapy, 2019)

When I'm clumsy, I haven't practiced or been exposed to an unfamiliar task or environment enough. Sometimes, though, my clumsiness is as a simple as being tired, stressed, and processing too much noise and stimuli. So the information about where I should be going next, and how I should be moving through space and time, gets lost in translation. When this happens, my brain shuts down and I forget what I'm doing and where I'm going. The closest possible comparison I can find is a video game analogy. My husband and I have dedicated hours of our lives to a video game called Cyberpunk 2077.

In Cyberpunk 2077, you often have the option of clicking the breach protocol button on lights, cameras, people, and massive automated guns. When you click the breach protocol button, a loading screen shows up. Then machines, devices, and people start to spin in confusion while electronic sparks fly. That's a great example of how my brain behaves when I get clumsy and oblivious to my movements, minus the flying sparks. Surface clumsiness is the result of a signal failing to reach my brain about the limitations of my environment, and resulting failure to react. Since people with an untrained eye cannot see what's going on, they will often oversimplify my experiences.

There's so much support that I still feel like I could use that is not yet available to me. Asking for and accessing support always gives me a massive amount of anxiety.

Chapter 12

The Impact of Having No Support

Dyspraxia is often left out of the disability conversation due to lack of awareness. At first, I thought awareness was exclusively a problem for Canadian dyspraxics. Then, I met a group of dyspraxics from five different countries. Dyspraxics from the U.S.A. and Australia talked about the level of awareness being minimal, and the challenges of accessing proper accommodations.

When I started to learn more about my condition, I gained a deep appreciation for the large number of resources available for dyspraxics in the U.K. For example, the British public health system (NHS) has an entire section on its website dedicated to dyspraxia. Despite the accessibility of important resources, many of the British dyspraxics that I've met were mistakenly labeled autistic. After extensive medical tests, they learned that they had dyspraxia.

Unfortunately, those unfamiliar with the condition don't understand what's going on inside the head of someone with dyspraxia. With disabilities like blindness, deafness, and other physical disabilities, there's an immediately obvious answer to what someone can't do. I'm physically fit, articulate, and well educated, so the severity of my condition is often underestimated. However, none of those things would have been achievable without the careful guidance of the educators who created an accessible learning environment.

In 1997, Hannah Palansky, a psychoeducational consultant, wrote the Toronto Board of Education document report[1] that gave me access to special education from kindergarten to my final year of secondary school. In the conclusion of that report, she discussed the true importance of her recommendations:

> *This delightful little girl requires intensive help to make academic progress. Specific fine and gross motor skills weaknesses, as well visual processing problems are undermining reading and math development. This assessment indicates some suggestions for working with Rosie at this time and changes in remedial techniques should be ongoing.*

Without the support that I received, I probably wouldn't have finished school, or gone to university, or written this book, or achieved any of the things that I have achieved so far. When dyspraxics can't access support, we cannot reach our full potential. When we cannot reach our full potential, we feel like a burden to everyone we care about.

Something we don't talk about enough—unequal access to care

In my adulthood, if I need occupational therapy or physiotherapy, I must pay for it, or meet narrow qualifications for subsidized care. Possible reasons for subsidized care include my need for therapy in the first place, where I live, work-related insurance that either I or my spouse qualify for, or how much money we

---

1   The report that I'm referring to is the IPRC (Identification, Placement, and Review Committee) report, which gives educators recommendations on what special education program is appropriate for students. This is an accommodation process that's available in Canada for young people with disabilities.

make. None of these reasons for subsidized care are a guarantee, especially in a household of independent contractors.

To receive disability support, you need to have a ton of self-awareness about your disability, but also need to know what to say to qualify for support. This is not something you can do alone. General practitioners (GPs) and bureaucrats are often required to fill out paperwork. They are often seen as trustworthy, but you can never assume that they'll understand, accept, or represent your diagnosis in a fair and accurate way.

In some countries and circumstances, accountants must get involved to file paperwork with your local tax office. If your case must be disputed, lawyers with experience working with disabled clients must get involved in the process. This creates a huge inequality issue, because the process required to access support creates barriers for people who cannot access the right people and resources.

Far too many dyspraxics are diagnosed in their adulthood and aren't guaranteed adequate support once they receive their diagnosis. Academia is always seen as an enlightened option for disabled people where they can receive diagnosis and support. However, proper support isn't a guarantee in any workplace environment. I have spoken to some dyspraxics in academia who tried to get proper support but had their support needs refused due to arbitrary, outdated rules and regulations.

An alarmingly high percentage of adult diagnoses and self-diagnoses have insufficient access to resources on how best to cope with their diagnosis. In our society, reasonable accommodations for people with invisible disabilities are treated like a luxury that you must reach an arbitrary idea of "being disabled enough" to be eligible for what you need to thrive. If you don't at least have the support of family, friends, or some sort of community to turn to, society's indifferent attitude toward disabled people can have a significant impact on your mental health and wellbeing.

A lack of support can lead to life experiences that are a lot like what Erin Gilmer faced on a regular basis. For such a long time,

Erin lived in poverty, and had chronic pain, along with multiple mental and chronic health conditions. She was estranged from her family and had no one local to talk to, but she had two cats that she loved dearly. On a regular basis, Erin offered support and guidance to disabled people who were being treated poorly by others. She was also a regular guest speaker at American political hearings about health policies that affected her, and a remarkable blogger. When I wrote and published a letter in response to *The Independent*'s negative portrayal of dyspraxia, Erin got me the support of several disability advocates.

In the summer of 2021, news spread amongst mutual friends of Erin's suicide,[2] and her death was a huge loss to everyone she advocated for. An article was published in the *New York Times* about Erin's life soon after her suicide (Risen, 2021), but she died with so little support that she thought that her life was meaningless. Unfortunately, Erin's story isn't an unusual one. The disability advocacy community has lost a lot of its most influential advocates for the same reasons.

Erin's story is also an illustration of just how insufficiently supported the hard work, creativity, and innovation of neurodivergent people can be. Since I was a kid, some progress has been made on including neurodivergent people in society; the level of support that's available is still a huge inequality issue based on factors no one has control over like where you grew up, and who your parents are.

Although self-diagnoses are taken seriously in the neurodiversity advocacy community, most medical practitioners require a formal diagnosis to recommend further treatment and care. Dyspraxics who got their diagnosis late in life or have self-diagnosed have told me that factors like the cost of the diagnosis are a huge barrier. Then there's the attitudes of family and your

---

2   If you are in crisis or suicidal and need someone to talk to, you can call the Samaritans branch in your area on 1(800)-273-TALK in the U.S.A. and 116-123 in the U.K. for free. Canadian readers have the option of Canada Suicide Prevention Service (833-456-4566), which is available for free 24/7, 365 days a year, with both English and French language options.

local medical team, which affect your likelihood of getting a diagnosis in the first place. Family, and sometimes even a dyspraxic's significant other, may not be willing to accept a dyspraxia diagnosis; they may be afraid of what others might think of a partner or family member's learning difference, along with the long-term effect on their loved one's future.

When doctors refuse to take dyspraxia seriously, it's usually a problem of lack of adequate resources. In some cases, the lack of resources situation is about lack of access to resources, lack of awareness amongst those seeking a diagnosis, and high price tags for diagnosis and relevant therapy in the first place. However, in some circumstances, the problem is that the person seeking a diagnosis has done credible research and asked for a second opinion of qualified professionals that validates their diagnosis, but their GP isn't taking their informed opinion seriously enough to make recommendations on what to do next. Sometimes this is the result of a lack of training for that specific physician about what dyspraxia even is, or what to do about it. I find, this can have mixed results. If the practitioner is open to learning as they go from their patients' experiences, they can learn from you and what you recommend. Although as I have mentioned in a previous chapter, there's not always a simple answer. If it's a doctor with a "my opinion is always the right opinion, do not question it" mentality, you're at the mercy of what they think unless you switch doctors. When these barriers are imposed, you don't have the piece of paper or level of understanding needed to get or ask for support in any setting when you need it. That's exactly when this starts to do horrible things to your mental health. You want to thrive and do as well as everyone else, but you can't because you can't get what you need to do that; that's when you start to feel frustration, resentfulness even, about your diagnosis and how it affects all aspects of who you are. In other words, education and relevant resources are a two-sided thing for all neurodivergent people to get what they need. It's tough to get support no matter how much is available in your area, but especially when everything from your local government to your doctors, educators, and employers aren't actively trying to educate themselves on how they can support you, and in some cases, not prioritizing these support programs in large-scale government budgets accordingly. Hours of emotional, unpaid labour are required to fill out relevant paperwork, sign up for and research support programs, and read articles and studies on your dyspraxia to know what your options even are. If individuals with the most influence and sway over neurodiversity and disability support programs aren't actively trying to learn more as well, far too many people's support needs will get swept under the carpet and ignored by "the system" itself, and that's never good. This is happening right now in some of the most developed and powerful countries in the Western world, where applications by far too many dyspraxic adults to disability support programs are denied.

I have also met plenty of doctors who refuse to learn about innovations and new findings in their field the moment they open their first clinic. Dyspraxia may be "just a phase" or "clumsiness" to someone's doctor, but that's often a sign that treatment and care will be refused. All those factors come with a depleted sense of self-esteem and self-worth.

For neurodivergence on a broader level, a lot of the general public, including a surprising number of medical professionals, often don't have a good sense of the difference between a symptom of being neurodiverse and a minor personality quirk. For example, I have heard people dismiss autism as "just being sensitive," ADHD as "not trying or hard enough, misbehaving, or being lazy," and dyspraxia as just "being clumsy." This often leads to people going all their lives, or most of their lives, without seeking diagnosis, support, treatment, or care of any kind, and not seeking answers about why they are how they are. It is simply assumed it's a character flaw above all else, because that point of view has never been challenged. Only sufficient resources can help address misconceptions about what neurodiversity looks like.

A lack of resources leads to a lot of people's mental health suffering as a result, since they assume their neurodivergent behavior is "their fault," and something they can stop doing (but aren't bothering to do something about). Lack of resources can also lead to people who suspect they have a diagnosis not seeking support because they don't know how, or don't know what subsidized programs are available if they cannot afford it. That's when they typically blame themselves in a harmful way for something that is clearly the result of neurodivergent characteristics. That self-blame makes people more prone to depression, substance abuse, and other related issues. I met a woman over Zoom once (she probably wouldn't be comfortable with my revealing her name or other details) who had so many stories of struggling with all the above because she didn't know she was dyspraxic until she was in her forties. If her kid hadn't got a diagnosis, she would never have known she was also dyspraxic.

Sometimes, having access to the right communities can help but that's also never a guarantee. Many disability communities rely on internet access and can't always accommodate other types of disabilities, like also happening to be deaf, blind, living in poverty, or being unable to speak. This immediately excludes people who either don't have internet access or are unable to communicate or understand other people in these communities, although these communities have been great for people who can't afford to or are unable to travel to a specific location.

However, for those who have managed to get a diagnosis, low self-esteem and self-worth can still be an issue. For many years, that was a huge struggle for me, because I didn't know anyone dyspraxic. Once I had a dyspraxic peer group, I had a much stronger sense of what's normal and abnormal for dyspraxics of my background and age group.[3]

---

3   If this is currently an issue for you, Chapter 16 has some practical advice and stories about joining and creating a dyspraxia support group.

The power and potential of the patient perspective

My husband is a founding trustee of an international type 1 diabetes charity, T1International. My strong writing and communications background and empathetic familiarity with the cause made me a perfect volunteer. Founder Elizabeth Pfister and I got to know each other through the social media and proofreading work I did for the organization. I have also been to Elizabeth's home in the U.K., stayed in the same Washington-based Airbnb, and we have explored the English countryside together.

One of the most important lessons Elizabeth's organization has taught me is the emotional sway of the patient perspective. In the summer of 2019, I went to a London, Ontario-based event that took place at the childhood home of Dr. Banting, the co-discoverer of insulin. Dr. Banting's childhood home is now a museum in London called Banting House.

Everyone involved in the event met up at a brewery in London afterwards. My most memorable experience at the brewery was when I met Nicole, an important figurehead for the charity's #insulin4all movement. Over the long term, she has been a valuable advocate for insulin access in America. Her son, Alec, died because he couldn't afford his insulin. He was 26 years old when he died, and the cause of death was insulin rationing. When my husband and I finally spoke to Nicole, I learned that the one thing that made her an expert was lived experiences. I always assumed that she had some sort of medical or academic training. However, she was something equally important: a mother overcoming her grief.

Nicole processed grief through getting the word out there about what happened to her son. She also attended protests and senate hearings about issues relating to insulin access. Nicole has challenged individuals who oversimplify and underestimate the severity of diabetes. In fact, she has spoken to policy makers who see diabetes as a lifestyle choice problem. Telling her son's story has helped people learn that about uncontrollable factors like genes and biology, and the importance of access to proper medicine and care.

If you're not in a position of power, you might be reading about the mental health costs of inadequate dyspraxia treatment and care and think that you're powerless. However, people like Nicole are proof that the average person can change the mind of politicians and people in positions of power. In fact, after months of telling the media and politicians Alec's story, Nicole got an emergency insulin bill passed in Congress, which is named after her son Alec.

Chapter 13

When Do People Need to Know About Your Dyspraxia?

Currently, we live in a world with a limited understanding of disability experiences. Some people are transparent about their lack of understanding, although there are just as many institutions that pretend to care because they want to improve their public image. Far too many workplaces hire people based on diversity rather than merit. When the diversity tick box is checked off, they feel like they've done their charitable deed for the year. As soon as disabled staff members request proper support, nothing happens.

This unfortunate reality makes finding the right time to tell people about your dyspraxia more complicated than it needs to be. For the first 13 years of my life, talking about my disability seemed taboo and terrifying. When I was in secondary school, I finally had a productive conversation about my disability with my best friend. She knew that I had a disability. When I talked about what I did and didn't find challenging, she finally understood what I was going through. Then she patiently helped in any way that she could.

Even though we're at a point in our lives where we're working adults with spouses, we keep in touch. She is now applying her love of helping others to her nursing job in The Hospital for Sick

Children's Cancer Wing. Her patients are children who are receiving cancer treatment, and it's the happiest I've ever seen her.

Telling my best friend about my disability was the supportive push I needed to have the same conversation with everyone else. Once I started university, I was a lot more strategic about when I talked to other people about my dyspraxia. When the people I spoke to were potential employers or professors, finding the right time or place to talk about my disability was challenging.

When I considered telling potential employers about my dyspraxia, I always thought that they would get rid of me and replace me with someone else. They might not have the resources to accommodate my needs. When I considered telling professors I respected about my dyspraxia, I had a severe mindset issue. I respected a lot of these people on an intellectual level, and I was eager to do well.

University was an opportunity to become a better writer and I was convinced that my professors could help me accomplish my goals. This made me really shy about discussing my disability with the people I considered to be potential mentors. An important mindset shift happened when a professor talked about his dyslexia. He focused less on provoking pity, and more on how his disability has helped other people. Struggling with learning how to read and write was a huge part of my childhood experiences with dyspraxia. So, hearing someone I respected talk about why they have a unique perspective on words inspired me to take accommodations a lot more seriously.

When I finally got help, I learned that getting support is socially acceptable. The more I talked to people, the more I learned that everyone had some sort of health issue (or will have some sort of health issue at some point in their lives). However, I don't think people should immediately walk around introducing themselves as their name followed by the word "dyspraxic," but I appreciate the comedy in this approach! When you act like it's your only personality trait, others will treat you like a one-dimensional character type.

When you're not treated like an equal, you won't have access to the same opportunities and experiences as everyone else. Equal opportunities require an equity-focused approach. A wise speaker at a conference I once attended described the difference between equity and equality as the following:

> Equality is when you give a disabled person a bike and tell them that they're welcome to ride that bike if they want to. Equity is when you redesign that bike based on what makes bike-riding accessible to a specific disabled person.

In other words, equality is about providing opportunity. Equity recognizes that everyone's circumstances are different, and we need to make accommodations based on what individuals need to reach a specific outcome.

On the news, I often see inspiration stories that foster an ableist attitude toward disabled people. A caring parent, grandparent, or relative talks about the challenges of taking care of a disabled person. Sad music plays, and the person with a disability is an object of pity. This perpetuates negative propaganda that says "people with a disability are a burden." Then, disabled people, along with able-bodied peers, internalize this logic.

Stories like these are a form of ableism because they trigger a toxic belief that disabled lives aren't valuable. Due to popular media narratives that foster this belief, disclosing your dyspraxia for the very first time is an uncertain and anxiety-inducing experience. When I was getting to know my husband's friends, I had to ask myself an important question: *How and when should I tell them about my disability?*

Every time I was invited to board games and beers social events, I had several opportunities to talk about what I could and couldn't do. Since I never focused exclusively on my dyspraxia, it was always a background presence. Eventually, I opted out of one of the games that were too spatial-processing-focused completely, but I was extremely apologetic about it. Then, someone within my husband's group of friends told me with a look of sincerity in their eyes, "I just want you to have fun."

I will never forget that moment, because it was the confirmation that I needed to feel like I had been heard, understood, and accepted. For far too long, I had an unhealthy obsession with finding the right time to tell people about my disability. There's no such thing as "the perfect time." You must be willing to take a leap of faith and tell people about your dyspraxia. It's a scary feeling, but the consequences of keeping your dyspraxia a secret are a lot worse. If you don't talk about your DCD, getting proper support will be unnecessarily complicated.

Chapter 14

Why Do Some Dyspraxics Avoid Driving a Car?

I never took my driving test, and I have never owned a car. Many of my relatives have told me that driving is a rite of passage, so I still face a great deal of peer pressure to get a license, something that seems unattainable.

For as long as I can remember, dyspraxia has given me a paralyzing fear of getting behind the wheel. On my second anniversary of being diagnosed, I realized that my mother had similar anxieties. In fact, she wasn't even comfortable with me jaywalking[1] on my own. At first, I didn't know what the fuss was about, but I took her advice seriously. Then I finally understood what she was so anxious about. All it took was a secondary school outing where I went out for occasional lunches with my friends.

One of my friends struggled with a variety of mental health issues and told me about her suicidal thoughts. As she asked me for advice, we jaywalked across a road. I got out of the way, but

---

1   After receiving input on my use of the word *jaywalking* from relatives in the U.K., I learned that jaywalking isn't really a "thing" in the U.K. Both Canada and America see crossing roads in high-traffic areas that don't have pedestrian crossing options (traffic lights and crosswalks) as a risky endeavor. In some areas, the consequences are a legal issue, in some areas there's a personal safety risk, and in some areas it's some combination of all the above. Regardless of the consequences, Canadians and Americans called it "jaywalking." However, Britain is more relaxed about it, and perceives safe road crossing as a personal responsibility thing.

she refused to get off the road, and I had to go back there to pull her toward the sidewalk. My anxiety about my friend's well-being put me in a position of stress, something that heightens the severity of my dyspraxia. When I'm stressed out, my ability to judge where I'm going and what's in front of me is worse than usual. Since I have poor spatial awareness, "worse than usual" means that it's non-existent.

I was so focused on my friend that I didn't see the truck coming in the same direction. As the driver honked their horn, I screamed, and both my friend and I ran toward the sidewalk.

That was the very first time I realized that on busy roads my dyspraxia can put me and others at risk. After that incident, I only jaywalked with other people. If I couldn't find someone I trusted, I followed strangers across the road who were jaywalking in the same direction. To this day, that's the only time I'll ever jaywalk.

One year after the jaywalking close call, I turned 16, the minimum age people can get their driver's license in Ontario. Although I knew that I could learn how to drive if I wanted to, I had no desire to get a license. It took me many years to realize that my mindset issues are my most significant barrier. When I re-read my Student Support Services IPRC report, I found a passage that perfectly expresses my mindset about things I can't do:

> During our assessment, Rosie was reluctant to perform puzzles and declined to do so. In class, occasionally when asked what activity she chooses, Rosie will state that she wants to do nothing. Her responses on these occasions appear to reflect some frustrations with motor tasks.

However, these frustrations tie into all other aspects of dyspraxia as well. I never learned how to drive because I know what I can't do. To operate a vehicle, you must quickly process the distance between yourself and other people. None of these skills happen as quickly or easily for a person with a dyspraxic brain.

I have met some British dyspraxics who drive, and many

of them deliberately avoid driving in London's downtown and high-traffic London commuter areas. Instead, they only drive in more relaxed medium- and low-density roadways outside of London. If you're not sure what's best for dyspraxic drivers in general, here's the most important lesson learned from a study conducted on a mixture of dyspraxic and non-dyspraxic drivers (Gentle et al., 2021): "Recognize the impact of both internal and external constraints on the ability of individuals with and without DCD to successfully interact with the environment."

I always knew that dyspraxia would make learning how to drive extremely difficult, but for such a long time I didn't know exactly why learning to drive is such an intimidating idea for me. Then I realized that my environment was a key barrier. I have always lived in noisy, crowded cities, and that gives me too many noises and people to focus on.

Riding a bike vs. learning to drive

Learning how to ride a bike broke my confidence in my ability to operate any kind of vehicle independently. Most of my peers learned how to ride a bike by their 8th birthday, and I learned how to ride a bike by my 13th birthday. It was one of the toughest things I have ever had to learn, and I have never been so fed up with the limitations of my body and mind. I would constantly bump into people, animals, and objects. I couldn't react fast enough or focus well enough to safely navigate high-traffic areas.

Eventually I got so fed up with how easily distracted my brain was that I gave up on riding a bike. After my parents sold my bike, we never spoke about bike riding again. Soon after I got rid of my bike, my parents got me a scooter, which was my main form of transportation until my third year of university. My scooter didn't have any engines or gears and weighed less than I did, so I couldn't do the same level of damage as a bike or car.

With a scooter, I could at least jump off quickly and have a firm grip on the handlebars if I lost track of where I was going and crashed into something. Learning how to ride a bike and a scooter was a huge accomplishment, but I never felt safe enough.

Urgency differences for aspiring drivers in big cities and small towns

Throughout my life, my strongest and most consistent coping mechanisms have always been necessity and urgency. If I must learn something that takes a bit longer for me to learn, I'll just keep trying until I figure it out. My determination only kicks in when it's a skill that I need to thrive in some aspect of my life.

I have never had to learn to drive or owned a car, because I have always lived in cities and neighborhoods with high walkability rankings. According to the Institute for Development Policy, the world's most walkable places are places where residents live within 100 meters of car-free spaces, such as parks, pedestrian areas, streets, and squares. Walkable cities are places where most residents live within a kilometer of healthcare and education (Carrington, 2020). Another key feature of walkable cities are small city blocks, where people can easily walk from one place to another without detours around large buildings. Whenever I have visited car-dependent places, I have always been able to find someone willing to drive me to where I need to go.

The first time I ever felt a sense of urgency about driving was when my husband and I were in Pembroke, Ontario, the small town he grew up in. Pembroke's walkability score, according to the WalkScore website,[2] is 37/100 due to its identity as a car-dependent city, and limited presence of bike lanes. So, every time we visit my husband's mom, we always rent a car.

One evening, my husband took us both out for a drive. In the middle of a quiet field with no one around, he let go of the wheel. Then he told me to take control of the wheel. Immediately, I started to scream. We were headed in the direction of a ditch.

---

2   www.walkscore.com/CA-ON/Pembroke

"Now, take us in the right direction," my husband said.

"But I can't. Stop it. This isn't funny," I remember saying.

"Yes, you can. Just listen to my instructions. Turn the wheel to the right," he replied, so calmly that I immediately followed the instructions. In only two tries on the steering wheel, I figured out which direction was right.

"Okay, now where do you think we need to go next?" he asked.

Instead of replying, I moved the car in the opposite direction of a nearby wooden pole. Then, the car moved forward because of my actions. As the car moved in the direction of a busy road, my husband gripped the wheel and said, "See? You can do it. You did it. Rosie...you drove a car...you actually drove a car!"

"Good for you," his mom replied from the back of the car, as my heartbeat got so fast that I could barely breath.

A key moment that helped me understand my dyspraxic brain

The second time I was in the passenger seat of a rental car, I tested out my dyspraxic brain by seeing how fast I could detect objects on the road. Throughout the car journey, my brain wouldn't detect crucial objects like ditches and wild animals until a few moments after we had driven by.

After trying everything from riding a bike, to riding a scooter, I learned that even a slow, casual stroll is something I can rarely do without bumping into things. I'm extremely prone to daydreaming so intensely that I forget or break things. I have always admired Jenny Hollander, a fellow dyspraxic writer's courage for having the confidence to take driving lessons. Not only did she try to learn how to drive, but she had the self-awareness to realize it wasn't for her: "I took 20 hours' worth of driving lessons before thanking my lucky stars for public transport and giving up. If there was an inanimate object in my neighborhood, I [would] probably hit it at some point" (Hollander, 2017).

What we need to make driving more accessible

Extra time and a quiet, alternative environment are needed for the written portion of the driving test. For dyspraxics, limited distractions make a huge difference. When too many instructions and distractions happen at once, many of us freeze and become a danger to others. Stress can also lead to the same results. In a vehicle, that's not something you can easily control.

Some driving schools in the U.S., Canada, and the U.K. specialize in drivers with disabilities, but once again we run into the issue of access. There's no actual guarantee that you will find an affordable instructor specializing in drivers with disabilities who understands and has the patience for dyspraxic drivers.

People give up too quickly on teaching dyspraxics how to drive, without asking themselves why. I once met a dyspraxic bus driver from the Canadian city of Thunder Bay. She drove for a living, accident-free, and was just as good a driver as her non-dyspraxic peers. Meeting her made me realize that learning, or not learning, how to drive is a choice that I can make at my own pace.

Making driving more accessible to dyspraxics requires better neurodiversity resources, and higher level of awareness about neurodiverse conditions in general. Once awareness starts to spread, more driving instructors will know what dyspraxic drivers need to be a safe and confident presence on the road.

Occupational therapy can help drivers with disabilities find adaptive equipment that allows them to drive. I have watched occupational therapists do amazing work, but it's the bureaucratic process itself that can be problematic. Many of the dyspraxia advocates I know in the U.K. have told me about British government programs that subsidize accessible equipment; these programs require applicants to navigate a lot of bureaucratic red tape.

You might know what you need, but the people with the power to decide what you can realistically access have their set of rules to follow. You're often placed in a difficult situation where you're either too disabled, or not disabled enough to access support.

For dyspraxic drivers, stigma is always a factor. Driving requires spatial awareness and coordination. Dyspraxic drivers require accommodations and strategies that help us work around a lack of spatial awareness and coordination. People often forget that we require support for driving because we seem independent and able. We're judged for not driving because driving is seen as a widespread symbol of independence. When we try to learn how to drive, practitioners often discourage driving altogether or don't consider the lifestyles of adults with DCD. Over the long term, this can lead to limited independence in cities that are designed with cars, not people, in mind.

Policy and infrastructure options worth considering
As much as I want to suggest having more public transport, I have been to places where cars are your only option, and it's never that simple. Building public transportation requires the cooperation of government representatives and residents of their communities, along with enough money and resources to build new infrastructure.

If we want to create neurodiverse-friendly cities and towns, everyone from bureaucrats to driving instructors needs good information about neurodiversity. However, proper resources aren't accessible enough to the average person. Power and short-term profits are often taken a lot more seriously than the needs of the average adult.

Instead of asking for policy changes that require influential politicians to think differently, I'm rooting for self-driving cars to get so good that they replace regular cars. If the artificial intelligence of self-driving cars gets extremely good, infrastructure will have to adapt to self-driving cars. The cars themselves will also have to be widely available, rather than marketed as Elon Musk's latest luxury invention.

If all the above happens, more people just like me will be on the road. There's a lot of skepticism about self-driving cars, but people cause accidents on the roads not machines.

Chapter 15

Traveling Abroad with Dyspraxia

By elementary school, I was already doing plenty of domestic and international travel via airplanes, boats, and trains to adapt to my family's travel-intensive lifestyle. My dyspraxia, though, has made travel...interesting, to say the least, because I regularly get lost and misjudge the amount of time required to get to my destination.

When all else fails, I rely on tools like Siri and Google Maps to provide a visual representation of where I should be going. Sometimes, I have tested the patience of GPS devices when I'm too tired, stressed, or distracted to understand the true meaning of turning left. I have had the voice of these devices practically scream the words "Turn left" several times in a row before I understand what that means.

I openly admit that my navigation tactics aren't perfect. Phones sometimes run out of batteries, but at least I can rely on my photographic memory. In the first article I ever wrote about my dyspraxia, I explained exactly how this memorization process works:

> My brain has developed a brilliant way to compensate for this challenge. I only have to navigate somewhere or learn an activity that requires complex fine and gross motor skills once; my brain will photographically memorize the steps required for the next occasion. (Richings, 2020c)

When none of my usual navigation tactics are working properly, I'll rely on other people or get immediately lost. Then, there are the spatial processing challenges, which get much worse when I'm tired or stressed, or there are too many sensory distractions.

Out of necessity, I learned a visual pattern that I often do when someone says "turn right" or "turn left," and my neurotypical family and friends aren't there to help me. Since I'm a native English speaker who can understand some French, I taught myself how to do this in both languages. If I ever learn more languages, the first thing I'll do is memorize the same sequence.

First, I move my right hand, and then my left hand in that exact order to remember which one is which. I memorized which one is which in order, and that makes a huge difference. Visual representations descramble my brain; that's a good thing because I frequently get confused about which direction is which. However, I still can't figure out east, west, north, and south, and can only figure it out if someone points in that direction or provides a visual demonstration of where I'm going.

In my hometown of Toronto, Canada, I can be in any neighborhood and tell you exactly where the lake is. Toronto's nearest lake, Lake Ontario, is a visual cue that local schoolchildren are taught so that they always know which direction is south. When I figure out where the lake is, I can always figure out which direction is north, west, and east. When I'm in another city or country, I don't have Lake Ontario to rely on, but I know what the North Star looks like. In case you didn't immediately guess this based on its name alone, The North Star is a brightly shining star that has a long tradition of providing travelers with a visual cue that says "North is this way."

How going to Halifax helped me gain the confidence to travel

When I was 16 years old, I traveled alone on an airplane for the very first time. I had no job, very little money in my bank account, and was too old for summer camp. So, my dad bought me a plane ticket to Halifax, Nova Scotia, a city on Canada's east coast. He was filming a movie, and no one wanted to leave me unsupervised. My mom was busy working, and the demands of being a student at Royal Military College made it impossible for my brother to spend time with me during March Break.

When I went to Halifax, my unreliable short-term memory, and tendency to lost track of important documents like my boarding pass, passport, and ticket, never stopped failing me. Many times in a row, I would panic and forget that these important documents were in obvious places like my pocket. Stressed-out airport staff were impatient with me, and they had to provide the same instructions several times.

However, a few kind-hearted stewardesses voluntarily helped me out. When I found out where I was supposed to be, the stewardesses kept an eye on me. Then, they made sure I knew exactly where I needed to go next. Eventually, I found my gate and stayed there until it was time for boarding. Once I found my gate, I had nothing to worry about. A few more times in a row, I forgot where I put my passport and boarding pass. When the plane landed with me on it, a driver for the cast and crew of movie my dad was working on picked me up at the airport. Then, they drove me to my dad's hotel.

Now, I keep all my travel documents in one place, so I panic less.

Jet lag in Paris

When my husband and I had only been a couple for about a year or two, we booked a flight from Toronto to Paris on Aer Lingus, an Irish airline. We planned our trip around spending some time in Paris and visiting my relatives in England, and then taking a return flight from Paris Charles de Gaulle airport back to Canada. When our plane left Toronto's Pearson Airport, the loud noises of the plane's economy class made it impossible to sleep. So, I listened to music and watched movies instead.

When we arrived at Dublin Airport, I kept myself awake with one of my greatest passions, language. I immediately noticed the widespread prevalence of one of the country's two official languages, Irish. Irish showed up on signs and on P.A. announcements. So, I turned the presence of the Irish language into a game meant to keep my brain alert. I listened carefully to the pronunciation of certain words and phrases and tried to guess what they meant based on the sounds of the words.

Once I was on the connecting flight to Paris, I had another chance to sleep, but I still didn't get any sleep. When we arrived in Paris, the number of things I had to process at once was a huge challenge for my dyspraxic brain. In fact, a lack of sleep makes dyspraxia a lot harder to manage. First, there was the prevalence of French. I have decent French comprehension but it's not my first language. So, I must put a lot of thought into what I say for native French speakers to understand me.

For a dyspraxic person, that's a lot to process; when I'm stressed, and sleep-deprived, I'll often physically and mentally freeze in place. Eventually, I'll regain enough awareness of my environment to move toward my destination, but that never happens quickly enough. On our first trip to Paris, my luggage got stuck in the automatic doors that activate when you put your ticket in the machine. Due to a lack of sleep, I couldn't form enough of a sentence to ask for help.

Fortunately, a friendly Frenchman pushed the bag out of the revolving doors. Before he rushed toward his destination, I managed to find the words to thank him. Once my luggage was finally in my hands, we had to find our train. When we eventually found it, the doors opened and closed far too quickly. Just in time, my partner rushed on board with the luggage. The dyspraxia took control as I froze in place, staring at the train I was supposed to get on. As the train arrived, my partner took my hand and pulled me in the direction of the train's doors. Once we found a seat, I fell asleep at last.

When the train arrived in downtown Paris, I had a moment

of triumph when I managed to order and pay for our meal in French. After our meal, my mind got a bit foggy, and I couldn't even process what was right in front of me. Cars honked, and pedestrians gave me annoyed, disgruntled looks.

Eventually, we found our Airbnb, a large apartment complex, thanks to my partner's proficiency in Google Maps. We asked random locals if they were our Airbnb host, and all we got were confused looks. At last, a young man in a France football shirt asked me to confirm that I was in fact the person who booked the space for duration of our trip. When I said yes, he gave us instructions about our Airbnb space in a mix of broken English and the occasional French word. Before he left, he gave us a complete tour of the space and then handed us our keys. I was still so tired that none of the instructions stuck, but an instructions/FAQs guide in multiple languages was there to help.

After the first international travel experience of my adulthood, I learned that there's no such thing as the perfect coping mechanism for travel. My perspective on travel quickly changed watching YouTubers like Gabriel Traveler and Indigo Traveller. Both YouTubers quickly learned that you can't escape jet lag, language and cultural barriers, and unexpected setbacks. All anyone can do is focus on getting to your destination and taking care of your most immediate needs.

Traveling to high-stimuli cities as a sensory sensitive person with DCD

After my trip to Paris, Moroccan cities like Casablanca and Marrakech seemed a lot more manageable. When I went to these two cities, I had to surrender to the fact that these cities are a stimuli overload—although the stimuli overload is what made these cities such a memorable experience. Multilingual merchants give a theatrical overview of what they sell and competed for the attention of passersby. Meanwhile, loud drum music and sounds of car horns fill the air. Powerful smells are everywhere, such as the smell of mint tea and fragrant spices.

The first time I went to Morocco, crossing the streets was an event. There was a minimal presence of traffic lights, and pedestrians didn't have the right of way. When you cross the street, you either must get out of the way of the moving cars, or risk getting hurt. The first time I went to Morocco, I learned to listen to my body when it was telling me that I needed to rest. That was an extremely important lesson for me, because staying focused in crowded areas drains my energy.

In Morocco, it's socially acceptable to ask taxi drivers, security guards, hotel staff, and people working in stores to help you carry bags and figure out where you need to go. If you want help, you must be willing to ask for it and tip people who make your life a little bit easier. If you're worried about the language barrier, a lot of local radio broadcasts and pop songs are designed with a multilingual audience in mind; that doesn't guarantee that you'll both speak the same language, but you can always try smartphone translation apps when neither of you is sure how to get your point across.

What I've learned about myself as a relatively experienced traveler

The more I travel, the more I feel brave enough to get lost and venture into unfamiliar places. There's a lot of evil in this world, but there are just as many good people willing to help passersby in need. Sometimes people will surprise you how much they're willing to help and look out for your best interests.

Some fear travel, but I see it as an opportunity to learn about myself, the world, and my greater purpose within it. All challenges are worth it in the end to learn something new. I thrive on patterns and routine, but I don't want to let that stop me from seeing what else is "out there."

My biggest issue with travel right now is that I get easily overwhelmed during the travel planning process. I prefer to either plan small details at a time or leave the planning up to someone else. It's more information than I can realistically absorb or remember. Fortunately, I'm surrounded by excellent travel organizers that are happy to narrow down their research to a few options. All the people in my life who are great at organizing trips have a gift for calmly explaining the pros and cons to me, and that's all I need to hear to be "travel-ready."

Chapter 16

Creating Your Own Dyspraxia Community

My dad has always looked out for one of my most important needs in my best interest: an ongoing need for community. Every time I start something new, he always asks me where I will find my community. I'm convinced that his emphasis on community has something to do with his professional background in theater and film, because it's a collaboration-based art form. Once I reached adulthood, he no longer had to tell me never to face bold, brand-new things alone.

The endless itch, however, to always be looking for a community got tougher and tougher to fulfill as a remote work lifestyle became a more central part of my life. When the COVID-19 pandemic started, my desire for community became something so much bigger. I had lived my life with dyspraxia for such a long time at this point, and I was so eager to meet more, like-minded dyspraxics.

It's hard to find resources that are relevant and written in English that's simple enough that you don't need a medical background or a Ph.D. to understand it. It wasn't until recently that I started to see doctors, academics, and therapists who ask the dyspraxia community for input on their work.

After interacting with a series of tweets that I found through a DCD conference's Twitter hashtag, I understood the academic and medical practitioner community a whole lot better. The most talked-about conference event happened to be the only event that featured input from dyspraxic adults about the most difficult parts of their lives. I was part of a large group of dyspraxic adults who spoke to the guest speaker ahead of time about what we found the most difficult. I talked about the stigma attached to having your disability misunderstood by everyone you meet. The rest of the community talked about dyspraxia and mental health.

Clearly, practitioners and academics understand that there are not enough resources for dyspraxics and their families. There are some good people out there trying to make dyspraxia-related information available to the average person. That's easy to forget when fighting for your right to be reasonably accommodated is a normal part of your life.

How to be a positive participant in the dyspraxia community

My first exposure to resources by and for dyspraxics was *Dyspraxia Magazine, Dyspraxia & Life Magazine,* along with Dyspraxic Help 4U,[1] Victoria Biggs's book *Caged in Chaos,* and Krystal Shaw's You-Tube channel about her own experiences with neurodiversity. Prior to that, the only groups I could find featured conversations from concerned parents of dyspraxic children. Although their intentions are good, parents often speak on behalf of a dyspraxic child.

Eventually, I started to collaborate with people like Billy Stanley of Dyspraxic Help 4U, Krystal Shaw, and the founders of the Dyspraxic Women's Network. Our biggest accomplishment so far has been creating a support network with a no-tolerance policy for bullying or harassment of any kind. Dyspraxic Alliance, an online support network by and for dyspraxics, was created with this purpose in mind.

We organize everything from dyspraxia-focused Q&As and (other) live streams to virtual social events. We also collaborate

---

1   www.dyspraxichelp4u.co.uk

with other independent advocates who are creating accessible resources and events for dyspraxics worldwide. However, we collaborate the most often with the Dyspraxic Women's Network, Dyspraxic Help 4U, and *Dyspraxia Magazine*. We operate as a larger collective to make all the above happen. Facebook is one component, but participants in our events don't necessarily have to have Facebook, because everyone involved tends to attract participants via our own individual, online, and offline networks which are growing gradually as we organize new events and projects. The organizers talk over Zoom on a regular basis about what we're doing next, and what we can all do to get the word out there about it before we announce our next project or event. We were all burning ourselves out trying to do everything alone. So, we tap into our own followings, resources, and networks whenever we develop new projects individually as well.

Most of the community are kind-hearted, wonderful people. The minority that are cruel to people who need support make it tough for dyspraxics to feel safe enough to share their experiences. As much as we want to help people, we are unable to help the community full-time. Many of us work, have families, and other health issues as well. We had to establish strict personal boundaries not to be treated like an unpaid therapist.

Despite some of the dyspraxia community in-fighting that I've seen, I really do believe that the community members need each other. This condition is heavily misunderstood, and the level of awareness isn't good enough. The hardest part is the little things. When you have no spatial awareness, fine, or gross motor skills, the jobs you can do, the people you can talk to, and the environments you can function in are frustratingly narrow.

To get something out of building my own community, I had to take what I wanted to get out of the hours of volunteer time into consideration. I had a much better experience when I realized that my ideal community is a place where participants support each other through all types of advocacy campaigns. Starting or joining a dyspraxia group is emotionally draining but fighting for the best interests of dyspraxics alone is a lot more difficult. Burnout is always the risk of trying to advocate alone, and that never leads to anything good. Especially when you're also juggling work and other responsibilities. Good people give up on advocacy when they're too tired and fed up to keep fighting and persevering.

Since you have read this book to the very end, I'm convinced that you're a person who wants what's best for dyspraxics in your community. The world needs more people like you, but you can't make the world a better place for dyspraxics alone. You need good, like-minded people who understand what you're going through.

Epilogue

I wrote this book to help people who are only just starting to comprehend their diagnosis (or the diagnosis of someone they care about). As I wrote it, though, I was also forced to reflect a great deal on aspects of my lived experiences that I overlooked or took for granted. When I look back at year one of my diagnosis, having immediate access to dyspraxia education and resources would have made finding what's best for me and seeking reasonable accommodations a lot less of a guessing game.

In the later stages of this book's development, my husband and I packed our bags and moved from Toronto to Morocco. Morocco is a country that can be a sensory sledgehammer at the best of times. So, managing to make that work, function semi-independently, and run a freelance business has created a lifestyle where I can exceed my expectations of what I can realistically do. None of that would have been possible without all the connections I established through the online dyspraxia community. Everything from being able to exercise virtually with a group of dyspraxics, to running events by and for dyspraxics didn't just help others just like me; it also helped me learn so much about myself from a global peer group with mutual questions and concerns. Roughly a decade prior to our big move, I chose to stay in Toronto for university. There was still so much that I didn't understand about my dyspraxia, and I was expected to figure out my accommodations needs on my own. Never in my life did I value my local health center, and the unconditional love of my family, more than I did back then.

I was afraid to leave the environment I found the most famil-iar, because I assumed that something would go horribly wrong because of my dyspraxia; I didn't know what that "something" was, but that's exactly what made it so terrifying. As I started to immerse myself in the dyspraxia community, I learned that I wasn't the only one who experienced symptoms that I cannot comprehend. Most of the online forum conversations start with the same question: *Is this symptom a normal dyspraxia thing?*

For dyspraxics to access lifelong reasonable accommodations, education needs to go both ways. Those who teach, work with, or live with dyspraxics need to know what to do when a symp-tom makes things difficult. Disclosing a dyspraxia diagnosis can be stigmatizing and intimidating, because not enough people understand what we're going through. Education and awareness can solve that problem.

Having access to education and resources about my dyspraxia as soon as I was diagnosed would have also made my quality of life a lot better. Now, I'm living a full and fulfilling life, but I can't help but wonder what I could have done if I had understood my dyspraxia much sooner. Perhaps I would have been able to work in a broader range of professions and environments as soon as I was old enough to work. Perhaps I would have received more than one university degree by my 30th birthday. Perhaps I would have been able to live alone at least once before I got married and had as much independence as my non-dyspraxic peers a lot sooner.

As I write this, I still have days when I feel like I am five years old again and trying to confront my dyspraxia symptoms on the first day of school. Having some of the healthiest, most meaning-ful relationships I have ever had, and having so many other good things going on in my life is what makes the hard parts worth fighting for. I mentioned in the introduction that I once felt like my family's greatest burden, but I'm happy to announce that I don't feel that way anymore. I worked so hard to overcome that hurdle and feel like an equal, and I hope that you or some other dyspraxic in your life gets to feel that way in the not-so-distant future.

For anyone just diagnosed, even if it feels like there is no local support in your community, there are resources and approachable dyspraxia advocates out there willing to offer guidance and support.

Acknowledgments

I want to start by thanking my husband James for being such a key source of support for this book. When I said "I want to write a book," his response was "Give one chapter a try, and if you want to keep going at this, just go for it!" Once one chapter became 16, he was my first ever reader. He never failed to give me a healthy dose of tough love, support, and occasionally a shoulder to cry on, during every stage of the process.

The rest of my family are also very important to squeeze in as well because they were advocating for me before I figured out how to advocate for myself. They gave me the strength to stick up for myself when I deserved better. As the book progressed, they were kind souls, offering to help in whatever way they could. That's an honor and a privilege that not everyone has.

I also cannot forget to thank Greg Ioannou of Iguana Books, who provided weekly mentorship on my book in its rough draft stages. Greg's mentorship was a healthy balance of being a believer in its true value, and a reality check.

On a similar note, I want to thank Susan Kernohan, the founder of my first ever writers' group. Susan was an influential figure who awakened my love of writing and provided a supportive environment that encouraged me never to stop exploring my own narrative voice. For that I'm forever grateful.

Glossary

ADHD: The U.S. Centers for Disease Control and Prevention defines ADHD as the following: "people with ADHD may have trouble paying attention, controlling impulsive behaviors (may act without thinking about what the result will be), or be overly active."

Advocacy: The process of not only publicly supporting a specific cause but providing recommendations on how best to support and improve the quality of life of people affected by a specific issue. For disability advocates specifically, everything from organizing events and creating resources to fighting for change in a specific government policy is an act of advocacy.

Americans with Disabilities Act (ADA): The ADA is an act that prevents discrimination against disabled Americans in all aspects of their public lives. Equal opportunity and access to accommodations are a core focus of the ADA.

Autism: According to Autism Ontario: "Autism affects the way a person communicates and relates to the world around them. It can affect body language and posture, social interactions and relationships, and sensory processing capacities."

Clumsy child syndrome: A term that predates the medical term for dyspraxia (DCD). This term is seldom used anymore due to its inaccurate portrait of what dyspraxics are going through. This was widely used back when all medical practitioners really knew about dyspraxia was that it makes children clumsy, affects their coordination, and interferes with their socialization and academic performance.

Dyslexia: Dyslexics have difficulty reading due to problems identifying speech sounds and learning how they relate to letters and words (decoding).

Dyspraxia (developmental coordination disorder: DCD): According to the *Dyspraxia Magazine* website: "Dyspraxia, also known as developmental co-ordination disorder (DCD), is a neurological condition that affects the brain's ability to process information. It results in disturbances in movements, planning, speech and learning new tasks/processing new information."

Equestrian therapy: Equestrian therapy, otherwise known as equine therapy, uses interactions with horses to provide therapy to people with physical and neurological disabilities. The core elements of equestrian therapy, which is heavily customized to suit the needs of a specific rider, are "feeling the physical cadence of a horse can stimulate one's muscles and spine. Horseback riding helps with motor skills, balance, coordination, and physical rehabilitation."

Hypotonia: According to the NHS: "Hypotonia is the medical term for decreased muscle tone. Healthy muscles are never fully relaxed. They retain a certain amount of tension and stiffness (muscle tone) that can be felt as resistance to movement."

Neurodivergent: This refers to any structured, consistent way that the brain works differently than it does for much of the population. All types of neurodevelopmental disorders (see the neurodiversity definition below), fall under this category, but so do mental health conditions such as depression, anxiety, OCD, and borderline personality disorder.

Neurodiversity: The idea that brain differences are just differences. They're simply variations of the human brain. Everything from ADHD, autism, dyspraxia, dyslexia, and Tourette's syndrome are celebrated forms of neurological difference, which are typically labeled "neurodevelopmental disorders."

Occupational therapy: Occupational therapists work with people of all ages helping them to overcome the effects of disability caused by physical or mental illness, aging, learning disabilities, or other factors. The aim is to enable people to carry out the daily activities, roles, and routines that are important to them.

Patient perspective: The patient perspective is the lived experience point of view. For disability resources with a patient perspective, a disabled person is sharing what living with their disability is like, and teaching coping mechanisms based on their own experiences.

Physiotherapy: The core goal of physiotherapy is restoring, maintaining, and making the most of a patient's mobility, function, and wellbeing. Physiotherapy guides you through physical rehabilitation, injury prevention, and health and fitness.

Self-advocacy: Looking out for the best interests of your disability, chronic illness, or overall health, and actively seeking accommodations and support that align with your own best interests.

Sensory processing: Sensory processing affects how your brain processes and responds to sensory stimuli (how things taste, smell, sound, and feel). People with sensory processing issues vary widely in terms of what they're sensitive to, and often experience distraction, anxiety, and an inability to focus or function in reaction to crowded or high-stimuli environments.

Stimming: The body language of both autistic people and neurodiverse people with other types of sensory disabilities. Hand flapping, rocking back and forth, spinning objects, visual stimming, auditory stims, verbal stims, and pressure stims are some of the ways it happens.

Wilbarger Protocol: The Wilbarger Protocol is part of a sensory therapy program. It involves brushing the body with a small surgical brush throughout the day. People who exhibit symptoms of tactile defensiveness are extremely sensitive to touch.

Bibliography

ADA National Network. (2019). 'What is the Americans With Disabilities Act (ADA)?' Information, Guidance and Training on the Americans With Disabilities Act. https://adata.org/learn-about-ada

Allen, S. & Casey, J. (2017). Developmental coordination disorders and sensory processing and integration: Incidence, associations, and co-morbidities. *British Journal of Occupational Therapy 80*(9), 549–557. doi:10.1177/0308022617709183

Arky, B. (2019). 'Supportive living for young adults with autism.' Child Mind Institute. https://childmind.org/article/aging-out-when-kids-with-autism-grow-up

Bascia, N., Fine, E., & Levine, M. (2017). *Alternative Schooling and Student Engagement: Canadian Stories of Democracy within Bureaucracy.* Toronto: Palgrave Macmillan.

Biotteau, M., Danna, J., Baudou, É., Puyjarinet, F., et al. (2019). Developmental coordination disorder and dysgraphia: Signs and symptoms, diagnosis, and rehabilitation. *Neuropsychiatric Disease and Treatment 15*, 1877–1885. doi:10.2147/NDT.S120514

Callahan, C. (2018). 'Aerie features models with Down Syndrome, insulin pumps in new lingerie ads.' Today Magazine. www.today.com/style/aerie-bra-ads-feature-models-disabilities-t133155

Canadian Civil Liberties Association. (2018). 'Workplace accessibility in Canada.' https://ccla.org/workplace-accessibility-canada

CanChild. (2020). 'What is DCD?' https://canchild.ca/en/diagnoses/developmental-coordination-disorder

Carrington, D. (2020, October 15). 'Study reveals world's most walkable cities.' *The Guardian.* www.theguardian.com/cities/2020/oct/15/study-reveals-worlds-most-walkable-cities

Cassidy, E. (2018). '"Doctor Who" includes new companion with dys-praxia.' The Mighty. https://themighty.com/2018/10/doctor-who-jodie-whittaker-companion-dyspraxia-ryan-tosin-cole

Dean, M. (2020, October 1). 'Finding your voice at work whatever your communication style.' [Blog post]. The Future Is ND. https://thefutureisnd.com/blog/finding-your-voice-at-work-whatever-your-communication-style

Department for Work and Pensions. (2021). 'Access to Work: Fact-sheet for customers.' www.gov.uk/government/publications/access-to-work-factsheet/access-to-work-factsheet-for-customers

Drmay, S. (2016). 'Up the disabled punx.' Broken Pencil Magazine. https://brokenpencil.com/features/up-the-disabled-punx

Dyspraxia Foundation. (2016). *Working with Dyspraxia: A Hidden Asset.* Cheltenham: Key 4 Learning. https://dyspraxiafoundation.org.uk/wp-content/uploads/2016/06/Employer_guide_to_dyspraxia_1.0.pdf

Dyspraxic Panda. (2015). 'Dyspraxic Panda: More about the admin.' Tumblr. https://dyspraxicpanda.tumblr.com/author

Engel-Yeger, B. & Segal, D. (2018). Sensory processing difficulties (SPD) and their relation to motor performance and to child's perceived competence among children with developmental coordination disorders. *International Physical Medicine Rehabilitation Journal 3*(2), 129–135. doi:10.15406/ipmrj.2018.03.00088

Gentle, J., Brady, D., Woodger, N., Croston, S., & Leonard, H. (2021). 'Driving skills of individuals with and without developmental coordination disorder (DCD/dyspraxia).' *Frontiers in Human Neuroscience.* doi:10.3389/fnhum.2021.635649

Government of Ontario. (2017). 'Get physiotherapy: Learn how you can get government-funded physiotherapy.' Healthcare in Ontario. www.ontario.ca/page/get-physiotherapy

Griffin Occupational Therapy. (2019). 'What is dyspraxia? It's more than just clumsiness.' www.griffinot.com/what-is-dyspraxia-myths-explained

Harris, S. R., Mickelson, E., & Zwicker, J. G. (2015). 'Diagnosis and man-agement of developmental coordination disorder.' *Canadian Medical Association Journal 187*(9), 659–665.

Hawthorne, L. (2021). 'How neurodiversity programs improve employee engagement.' Uptimize. https://uptimize.com/neurodiversity-engagement

Hollander, J. (2017, May 19). '27 signs you may have dyspraxia.' Bustle. www.bustle.com/p/27-signs-you-have-dyspraxia-aka-developmental-coordination-disorder-58912

Kirby, A. (2021, August 26). 'Is there a link between neurodiversity and mental health?' *Psychology Today*. www.psychologytoday.com/gb/blog/pathways-progress/202108/is-there-link-between-neurodiversity-and-mental-health

Laitner, S. (2016). 'The hidden workplace skills of those with dyspraxia.' *Financial Times*. www.ft.com/content/b4255c98-ca7a-11e5-a8ef-ea66e967dd44

Missiuna, C., Gaines, R., & Soucie, H. (2006). 'Why every office needs a tennis ball: A new approach to assessing the clumsy child.' *Canadian Medical Association Journal* 175(5), 471–473.

National Autism Resources. (2021). 'The Wilbarger Protocol (brushing) for sensory integration: Helping people sensitive to touch.' https://nationalautismresources.com/the-wilbarger-protocol-brushing-therapy-for-sensory-integration

NHS. (2021, September). 'Overview: Hypotonia.' www.nhs.uk/conditions/hypotonia

Ontario Society of Occupational Therapists. (2020). 'Who pays for OT services?' https://otontario.ca/understanding-ot/funding-for-ot-services

Reaume, A. (2019, June 6). 'Interdependence as disabled poetics and praxis: Or why my novel is dedicated to my disabled friend Maddy.' Open Book. http://open-book.ca/Columnists/Interdependence-as-Disabled-Poetics-and-Praxis-Or-Why-My-Novel-is-Dedicated-to-My-Disabled-Friend-Maddy

Richard, O. (2016). 'A "button breakthrough": How dance therapy helps teen with disability. AZ Central. www.azcentral.com/story/news/local/phoenix/2018/02/03/button-breakthrough-how-dance-therapy-helps-teen-disability/1087500001

Richings, R. (2019a). 'The 7 best tips for sleeping with back pain.' Saatva: Sleep Enlightened. www.saatva.com/blog/best-way-to-sleep-with-back-pain

Richings, R. (2019b, November 4). 'The true story behind my fondness for mediation.' Medium Digest [Blog post]. https://medium.com/@rosierichings/the-true-story-behind-my-fondness-for-meditation-92669b8f54eb

Richings, R. (2020a, November 10). 'The challenges of staying fit as a neurodiverse person.' Medium Digest [Blog post]. https://rosier-ichings.medium.com/the-challenges-of-staying-fit-as-a-neurodi-verse-person-9bad3f3ddda6

Richings, R. (2020b). '5 essential ways to accommodate disabilities at work—including invisible ones.' The Good Trade. www.thegood-trade.com/features/mindful-work-accommodations

Richings, R. (2020c, September 21). 'Living with dyspraxia.' Medium Digest [Blog post]. https://rosierichings.medium.com/living-with-dyspraxia-9a2f10ad7fc4

Richings, R. (2021, April 9). 'According to *The Independent*, people with dyspraxia are slow underachievers but that's not true.' Medium Digest [Blog post]. https://rosierichings.medium.com/according-to-the-independent-people-with-dyspraxia-are-slow-underachiev-ers-but-thats-not-true-c8c22c238005

Risen, C. (2021, July 17). 'Erin Gilmer, disability rights activist, dies at 38.' *New York Times*. www.nytimes.com/2021/07/17/health/erin-gilm-er-dead.html

Rudy, L. (2020). 'What is sensory processing disorder?' VeryWell Health. www.verywellhealth.com/what-is-sensory-processing-disorder-260517

Silberman, S. (2016). *Neurotribes: The Legacy of Autism and the Future of Neurodiversity*. New York: Avery.

Turner, L. & Andrew, N. (2020). *Dyspraxia in the Workplace: Thinking Differently at Work*. London: GMB Union. www.gmb.org.uk/sites/default/files/neurodiversity-dyspraxia-guide.pdf

Index